"I have known Layla Palmer in her fearful days and her fully alive days, and the truth is we all exist somewhere in between. Coming Home feels like an exhale after holding your breath for far too long."

CARLOS WHITTAKER, author of *How To Human*

"Layla is a voice for personal over perfection in our homes, and her honesty about the truest comforts being found in our people and their stories will resonate with introverts and homebodies like me."

ERIN NAPIER, host of HGTV's *Home Town*

"*Coming Home* is like a vintage treasure. It is quietly wise and sweetly delightful. I will be dipping into these comforting pages again and again because we all need a little help finding our way home."

CHRISTIE N. PURIFOY, author of *A Home in Bloom*

"In *Coming Home*, Layla's storytelling is warm, rich, and vulnerable, drawing you into her world and making you feel less isolated in your own. Reading this book felt as familiar as settling in with an old friend on a front porch swing.... Layla's words wrapped around me like a soft and cozy, hand-knit blanket."

JENNY MARRS, co-host of HGTV's *Fixer to Fabulous*, author of *House + Love = Home*

"For many years, Layla has inspired my longing for a cozy, physical home where I can nurture myself and my family. But now in her book, *Coming Home*, she has inspired a deep longing to create that cozy home feeling inside of me instead, so that no matter where I am in this world or what challenges

I encounter on this journey of life, I won't lose myself, and I will always feel at home."

LIZ MARIE GALVAN, author, blogger, and shop owner

"In *Coming Home*, Layla Palmer eloquently traces her personal journey to discovering her authentic self—her home—within and without herself. Beautifully told through vignettes, photos, notes, and favorite quotes, *Coming Home* will find a place in reader's hearts, and on their bookshelves of favorites. I know it will find a treasured place in mine."

MARY KAY ANDREWS, *New York Times* bestselling author of *The Homewreckers*, *The Santa Suit*, and more

"This entire book is one giant exhale. I can't think of anyone who doesn't need it."

LISA-JO BAKER, bestselling author of *Never Unfriended* and *Surprised by Motherhood* coming home

Previous books by Layla Palmer

The Happy Crab with Kevin Palmer

coming home

A ROADMAP FROM FEARFUL TO FULLY ALIVE

LAYLA PALMER

BETHANYHOUSE
a division of Baker Publishing Group
Minneapolis, Minnesota

© 2023 by Layla D. Palmer

Published by Bethany House Publishers
Minneapolis, Minnesota
www.bethanyhouse.com

Bethany House Publishers is a division of
Baker Publishing Group, Grand Rapids, Michigan

Printed in China

ISBN 978-0-7642- 4077-5 (cloth)
ISBN 978-1-4934-4219-5 (ebook)
Library of Congress Cataloging-in-Publication Control Number: 2023009157

The information in this book is intended solely as an educational resource, not a tool to be used for medical diagnosis or treatment. The information presented is in no way a substitute for consultation with a personal health care professional. Readers should consult their personal health care professional before adopting any of the suggestions in this book or drawing inferences from the text. The author and publisher specifi-cally disclaim all responsibility for any liability, loss, or risk, personal or otherwise, which is incurred as a consequence, directly or indirectly, of the use of and/or applica-tion of any of the contents of this book.

Unless otherwise noted, all photos are by Layla and Kevin Palmer.

Cover design by Studio Gearbox
Cover photography by Kyle Campbell @SuddenJourneys
Interior design by William Overbeeke

The author is represented by Alive Literary Agency, www.aliveliterary.com.

23 24 25 26 27 28 29   7 6 5 4 3 2 1

For the person opposite this page . . .

Remember:
Home isn't just a somewhere
or a some-who,
home is also (and mostly)
the latitudes and longitudes
of you.

I Shall Write
a Book Some Day

I shall write a book some day,
Thin and flexible as leather;
A few sheets of tissue-thin
Paper bound together.

But my flattened heart will lie
Quietly between those bindings,
Crushed and squeezed and written out
With its ardent findings.

Just a slender little book,
Edged with gold, its stanzas fired
From the embered core of life;
But when hands are tired

They can hold my little book;
Failing eyes can read it,
And there will be something there
For the hearts that need it.

—Selected[1]

coming home is . . .

contents

introduction

I'm a writer, and everything I write is both a confession and a
struggle to understand things about myself and this world in which
I live. This is what everyone's work should be—whether you dance or
paint or sing. It is a confession, a baring of your soul, your faults,
those things you simply cannot or will not understand or accept.
You stumble forward, confused, and you share. If you're lucky, you
learn something.

—Arthur Miller

Every once in a while, we'll be moving through life,
and something traumatic will happen that completely derails us. For me, it was a burgeoning battle
with generalized anxiety that slowly, and then very suddenly,
erupted into a daily struggle with panic. And although I'm
still learning how to not react, here's something I know now
that I wish I had known back then: When it comes to the
slippery slope of overwhelming fear, if you're not intentional
about getting back on the road, you run the risk of only sliding sideways. Because when you mostly only work hard to
avoid the thing that knocked you off your path, you also stop
moving *toward* the things that make you come alive.

I was sitting in the passenger seat of an extremely loud and bouncy rental RV when my husband, Kevin, asked me the question that eventually led to the creation of this book. It was late October 2018, and we were driving back to Alabama from my home state of Minnesota. I had whipped together the semi-spontaneous adventure because I thought going "home" might help me escape an unrelenting season of panic and anxiety. It didn't work though, and as I headed back "home" to Alabama I felt just as lost as I had when I left.

"If not Alabama, and not Minnesota, where is home then?" Kevin's question instantly triggered tears because I didn't know how to answer. I realized I didn't feel safe anywhere anymore. Not even inside myself.

I had set out on that trip so hopeful that a visit with my relatives would help me reset. I was so sure that I could find peace in the people, places, and pastimes that had brought me so much joy before disordered panic. But I couldn't. Familiarity couldn't fix me, and I left Minnesota feeling more hopeless and afraid than ever.

But I know now, some five years later, that when it came to that trip — like so many other times I had struggled with fear of fear—I had my eye on the wrong destination. My predicament wouldn't ever be cured by rushing off to a "safe" place or by surrounding myself with "safe" people. Because I wasn't struggling with a physical location. I was struggling with a physical *sensation*. It was an inside issue. And you can't run away from yourself.

For the longest time, I regretted going on that trip. I struggled with agoraphobia at almost every stop, and I felt embarrassed that I couldn't be fully present with my family.

CAMP WANDAWEGA - OCTOBER 2018

The difference between me and everyone else created a chasm that seemed unspannable.

But now that I've had more time to process and grow, I can see that coming home isn't a thousand desperate miles between internal sensations and external safety. **The journey of coming home is measured in feet. It's taking one brave step, and then another brave step, until the steps don't feel so scary.**

That's what this book is all about: coming home. It is my own circuitous journey—a road I'm still learning how to surrender to—and a place of respite and inspiration for *you*, as you continue coming home to yourself too. And as I tenderly typed out each heartfelt word, I imagined us sitting together at one of my favorite places on the planet: our house. It's an oldish brick number, with squeaky doors and patchwork floors, and it's surrounded by a six-acre pasture that, somehow, feels directly connected to my pulse.

Sometimes I sat at my desk upstairs by the window that overlooks our land. Sometimes, I curled up on the couch in the living room or on one of the recliners in my mother-in-law's "snug." But, either way, I wrote the whole thing as if you were right here with me. Oftentimes, I recorded a voice note to myself, saying whole sections out loud, hoping that if I typed it down exactly the way I said it, you'd feel like you were here while you read it.

And now that this conversation starter has come together for keeps, I can share with you that **Coming Home is a kaleidoscope of things, really, but in a nutshell, it's a big-hearted book about feeling lost sometimes, and how to keep coming home.** Because don't we all lose our way every now and then? And isn't home more than just a place on a map? I think home is also (and mostly) a feeling *inside* of us. The warmth in our spirit. The sum of our strata. The source of our dreams. A sigh of relief.

> Home is where we tie one end of the thread of life.
> —MARTIN BUXBAUM

But when we get disconnected from the home of who we are, life within our skin can start to feel really uncomfortable and off-balance. We make a lot of sudden movements—or no movements at all. We overthink everything and tie our willpower to our worth. We lose touch with capable, cut out for, and courageous. We experience ourselves as inadequate. The scale often lunges toward unequipped, afraid, alone, and/or stuck.

I know those feelings well. In 2018, shortly after becoming a mom to our then-six-year-old son, and while my husband was on a mission trip in Haiti, I had a terrifying panic attack that dramatically altered the trajectory of my life. The experience unleashed a fear of fear itself, and when my hormones began to go haywire a few years later, menopause made handling stress even more challenging.

Thankfully, I have learned that time really *can* be a benevolent healer, and that leaning into the discomfort that comes along with fear is always more helpful than avoiding it.

> I'm learning to make things nice for myself. Slowly building myself a home with things I like. Colors that calm me down, a plan to follow when things get dark. A few people I try to treat right, even though I don't sometimes, but it's my intention to do so. I'm learning. . . .
> I'm trying, as I always will.
>
> —CHARLOTTE ERIKSSON

I have also discovered that sometimes, all it takes is one radically authentic conversation with one warmhearted person to reignite the kind of inner fire that can help put you on the path back home. I truly hope the voices in this book serve as that kind of guide for you.

Coming Home is a collection of essays (personal stories with helpful/hopeful takeaways) and extras (things like lists, recipes, doodles, poems, and quotes).

These are my ups and downs, joys and sorrows, fears and glimmers of hope. These are the stories that have shaped who I am today and the places that are a part of my history. (Some of them just don't know it yet—ha!) These are the quotes, or "distilled genius" as the incomparable Susan Branch would say, that have suffused my soul and that enlighten my life like sunbeams whenever I reread them.

> Discovering the collected knowledge of our ancestors provided me with an education like no other and shined a light on my possible path in life at a time when I was upside-down and backwards. . . . A gift like no other.
>
> —SUSAN BRANCH

Like Susan, I have been collecting quotes for as long as I can remember. Scribbling them down on whatever is handy *with* whatever is handy at the time—nothing is off-limits! Many of the words of wisdom I've saved along the way have been life-shaping, and I named my blog "The Lettered Cottage" for that very reason.

In *Coming Home* are the hand-drawn illustrations "clamoring to become visible"[1] on paper canvases that wanted more than just words. As a child, I always believed I'd be an artist when I grew up, so I guess the doodles in this book are also a nod to that age-old dream.

These are the recipes that taste like home, contributed by some of the people who feel like home, because I believe comfort food (and comfort people!) really are a "heart's astonishment."[2] If you decide to give any of our dishes or desserts a whirl, I hope they feel like family to you too.

One of the voices in this book belongs to my husband, Kevin. Don't worry, he's a really kind and insightful guy. ☺
You'll know it's him speaking whenever you see this notebook paper. (Each of his sections will be labeled From Kevin.)

These are the handwritten notes that I scribed especially for you, in hopes that experiencing pen on paper (not just pixels and print) will help us forge a deeper connection; I wanted each page to hold and to hear so much.

These are the little steps of courage that led me back to myself, and the soul-centering navigational tools I acquired along the way.

Coming Home is a map—overflowing with reminders about the BIG, important magic that can come from very small and precious things—created to guide you back to the treasure that will always be *you*. And I'm sharing all of this because you are probably handling *hard* better than you're giving yourself credit for. And maybe you need to be reminded that you are not your worst days; you are not whatever happened to you. You are a paradox, and your head and your heart are designed to ebb and flow with a more complicated mix of emotions than you might think. Both/and is *normal*, no matter what you've always been told. There is room for both optimism and anxiety, both hospitality and hesitancy. Both goosebumps and grief, both peace and plumb tuckered out. **There is room for both coming home and the unknown.** Because when it comes to experiencing emotions, both/and really is the trademark of living fully alive.

But before you go thinking I've got it all figured out, here's something else I need you to know about me and this book: I didn't write it from a place of arrival. I haven't crossed a finish line marked "fixed". (Spoiler alert: I'm not broken.) These stories sprang from a place of necessity and contain some of the things I've learned that have helped me. *Coming Home* is me not giving up and the truths that have kept me afloat.

> Do not think that the person who is trying to console you lives effortlessly among the simple, quiet words that sometimes make you feel better. His life is full of troubles and sadness and falls far short of them. But if it were any different, he could never have found the words that he did.
>
> —RAINER MARIA RILKE

And although I feel afraid to allow some of my wounds to go on existing in this way—like pressed flowers between pages, complete with their roots and thorns—I hope that by sharing them, they will leave the kind of mark that proves adversity (and achievement!) aren't ever unique to just one person. More than anything, I hope they will help *you* move forward on hard days too.

> You think your pain and your heartbreak are unprecedented in the history of the world, but then you read. It was Dostoevsky and Dickens who taught me that the things that tormented me most were the very things that connected me with all the people who were alive, or who had ever been alive.
>
> —JAMES BALDWIN

So, whether it's because of fear, insecurity, depression, grief, (menopause!) or some other uncomfortable emotion that has slowly (or suddenly) come between yourself and living fully alive, think of *Coming Home* as a buoy that just happens to look like a book. I hope that every time you reach for it, the good intentions and (often hard-won) truths inside will help keep you afloat and leave you so full of hope there won't be any room for the opposite to get in.

And just like that, we're on our way to everywhere.

—EMERY LORD

a note about the bones of this book

Because coming home to oneself isn't a set-in-stone, one-size-fits-all kind of adventure (and who am I kidding? I've always leaned more loosey-goosey than laced up!), I wanted this book to flow to the beat of its own format. So inside, you won't find traditional, back-to-back chapters. Instead, you'll discover a flexible collection of essays and extras. The first essay will give you some context about my personal struggle with panic (Buckle up! It's a doozy!), but feel free to throw a dart at the map (er, book) and jump into the journey wherever you'd like. Every page is meant to plant a seed; every word is intended to connect a dot. Because *Coming Home* (both the book and the metamorphosis) is less about becoming a *new* person, and more about coming home to the person who has been there all along. Coming home is the efflorescence of *you*.

efflorescence

noun | ˌe-flə-ˈre-sᵊn(t)s

the action or process of
developing and unfolding as if
coming into flower : BLOOMING[1]

coming home is . . .

the warrior in our bones

*Only when we are brave enough to explore the darkness
will we discover the infinite power of our light.*

—Brené Brown

I've always had trouble sleeping alone at night. I don't know exactly why, but as David Benioff wrote, "I've always envied people who sleep easily. Their brains must be cleaner, the floorboards of the skull well swept, all the little monsters closed up in a steamer trunk at the foot of the bed."[1]

As a young girl, I spent as many nights as possible at my Grandma Evelyn's house because she would always hold my hand until I fell asleep. She didn't share a bedroom with my Grandpa Richard (seems like it had something to do with his snoring), so her room was set up strictly for us girls. We each had our own twin-sized bed, and I can still feel the raised patterns on her heavy, chenille bedspreads if I think hard enough about them. Her curtains were lace, of course, and the large porcelain lamp on the nightstand between our beds featured a rouge-cheeked Victorian couple holding hands beneath a bell shade wrapped in gathered tulle. The dressers were mid-century modern in style and held so many of my grandma's favorite things. The top drawer of the longest dresser was full of her costume jewelry, all neatly organized in little, batting-filled cardboard trays.

My favorites were her brooches—fancy, ornamental pins encrusted with gemstones of every size and color. I was always intimidated by the big, hinged needles that stretched across the back, but boy did I feel like an actual princess holding that many jewels in my little hands! The ones with clear crystals were great for your garden-variety special event, but the colorful ones *really* made a statement on extra-special occasions. Especially the butterfly. Even resting next to all the other brooches, the butterfly always seemed to stand out. Sometimes, I'd pull the drawer open just so I could sneak a peek at its wings. They were filled with the happiest colors—periwinkle, jade, lavender, tangerine, and bubblegum pink—all outlined by seventy smaller, iridescent stones. It almost couldn't help but shimmer, whether it was pinned to a person or not.

My grandma passed away in 1999, but the butterfly sparkles on in my own home now. I keep it in a top drawer just like she did, and its pretty wings still whisper the same message they always have: *It is your grandma who makes me so special.*

I don't know how long I have been asleep, but my eyes just shot open, and I feel disoriented and wildly afraid. The room is pitch black, except for the light seeping out around the bathroom door. I always leave that light on when my husband, Kevin, is out of town. Or in this case, headed out of the country. A few of the caseworkers at our adoption agency asked me to help organize a mission trip to Haiti, so I encouraged Kevin and a few friends to go. I am passionate about helping folks in need, and that little island will always hold a special place in my heart. But now there is a suffocating weight bearing down inside my chest, and my heart is pounding frantically against it. *Am I having a heart attack?* The thought catapults me upright. I feel like I need something underneath my feet, but my equilibrium is off and the floor pushes back as if it doesn't want to hold me. *Was I having a nightmare before I was suddenly awake? What is happening right now? Am I about to die?* The past, present, and future suddenly exist as a single, crushing force.

My six-year-old son, Steevenson, is asleep next to me. This is our first night alone (without Kevin) since we adopted him eighteen months ago. I reach out with trembling hands to find my phone on my bedside table. It flashes 12:10 a.m. when my fingers graze the screen. *Ugh.* Nighttime always feels like such a countdown. So many hours between bedtime and feeling safe.

Kevin's parents moved in with us a couple of months ago, and in this moment of terror and confusion, I suddenly have a moment of clarity: *Go get Katie.* In a fuzzy flash, I am downstairs in my in-laws' bedroom, praying Steevenson doesn't wake up while I'm gone. My father-in-law is snoring in his recliner as I hover over my mother-in-law, Katie, who is fast asleep in her bed. The room feels otherworldly, almost like it's too dark to hear and too loud to see. I rock back and forth, bent forward with my hands on my knees in a desperate effort to release some of the tension. I lean in closer and whisper, "Mom," but her name is gobbled up by the whir of the air conditioner. She is still lying flat on her back and motionless; my father-in-law also hasn't shifted. I am embarrassed on top of afraid. A helpless feeling floods through me, kind of like when you're swimming and you move to put your foot down, but the water is deeper than you thought and there's nothing down there to hold you. I whisper, "Mom," a little louder and wait for her eyelids to move. When they do, she is confused and begins to shrink backward, like I'm armed with a taut rubber band aimed in her direction. I rush to help her understand.

"IjustwokeupbecausemyheartisracingsofastandIdon't knowwhat'sgoingonbutit'sbeatingsofastandIdon'tknowwhat todobutmyheartisjustracingsofast." The words rocket out like a poorly packed parachute—messy and with zero resistance. She is half asleep but rises from the bed so we can move to another room to talk. In the kitchen, I describe my symptoms again. I can tell that she is groggy and unsure of how to help, so I ask her if she thinks I should take a Xanax. She says, "Yes, if that's what they're for . . . then, yes, I think you should take one." But I am hesitant, because pills scare me too. I had a traumatic allergic reaction to codeine in my twenties, and I've been reluctant to take any kind of medication or painkiller since. "Maybe I'll just take a half," I say, curling the end into a question so she has to encourage me again. "Yes," she says and moves toward the cupboard that holds our cups and glasses. "Okay," I reply while vibrating over to my purse.

. . . Katie is sitting up on Kevin's side of our bed now, and I am lying down on the other side of Steevenson. I want her with us until the Xanax kicks in. *Sure, I've taken it a few times before, but what if I'm allergic all of a sudden? What if someone accidentally (or intentionally) laced this particular batch with something else?* I am an uncapped hydrant of irrational thoughts. I would hold my mother-in-law's hand right now, if she invited me to grab it.

A half hour or so has passed. Steevenson is still asleep between us (thank God), and Katie wants to know if I'm doing okay. I say, "I think so," and she tells me she really needs to go back downstairs. Sometimes, Jim loses his balance when moving between his chair and his scooter, and she wants to be down there in case he needs help. I understand, but something inside me still doesn't feel safe without a grandma.

Thirty minutes later, I am asleep.

. . . The sun is up now, and Steevenson and I are sitting side by side on our golf cart as it climbs up the dusty hill that flattens out at the school. I am holding myself together, but I feel brittle and bewildered. *Is there something critically wrong with my heart?*

I call Dr. McLaughlin's office when I get back home. I leave a message at the tone, and his nurse calls me back a few moments later. She tells me to come in at 11 a.m. I tell her that I usually take a Xanax before going to any kind of medical appointment but, of course, I make the mistake of asking her if she thinks I should. She says no, and I feel equal parts apprehensive and relieved.

Katie drives me to the appointment and sits next to me in the waiting room. There is an old-school clock on the wall, and for some reason, I find comfort in its familiar face. It looks like the one in Ms. Johnson's classroom. She was my art teacher in elementary and high school, and I spent as much time as possible creating things in her room. The clock's sweeping hand holds my attention for a minute, but the intrusive thoughts boomerang back as I begin to lose interest. I tell Katie that I feel lightheaded, so she stands up and moves toward the receptionist to tell her I might need to lie down. There are only a handful of other patients waiting in this room, but every one of them is looking at me now. The middle-aged man sitting straight across from me is smiling like he understands, so I smile back and shrug as I fan my red face with my hands.

A busy nurse is forced to usher us into the only room available. It is small (maybe six by eight feet?) but the wall opposite the door is mostly glass, and I am thankful for the sun-dappled view. I climb onto the examination table and hug my purse hard, as if it is supposed to be a permanent part of me. My mother-in-law looks concerned but pats my leg like she's certain there's no real reason to be. "Just calm down," she says. I am distracted momentarily by the glossy green oak leaves shimmering in the breeze behind her, and for some reason, the flickering of sunshine and shadows serve as a friendly reminder. *I have a holy spirit.* The thought drifts into my mind like a familiar train pulling into an unfamiliar station.

The nurse comes back to check my blood pressure. The top number is 150-something and with raised eyebrows and wide eyes, she too suggests I calm down. Her expression makes my pulse race even faster. On her way out the door, she assures us that the doctor will be along shortly, but a more fatal narrative has already snaked tightly around me, and now I am certain my mother-in-law will be the only one here when I finally succumb to a stroke.

By the time the doctor comes in, I can't feel the left side of my face, and a new level of terror has overtaken me. I beg him to "Please help me!" and he, too, tells me to "just calm down." But decelerating doesn't even feel like an option at this point. Because somewhere inside me, a pressurized floodgate has finally burst open, and adrenaline is rocketing through my veins. I am ice cold and trembling hard against the current when I feel a zip tie close tight around my windpipe. I gulp frantically for air, but because that passage is clamped shut, none of it reaches my lungs. My body has forgotten how to breathe. My senses heighten to the point of paralysis, and both of my hands involuntarily curl in. I can see that they're attached to my body, but it feels like they belong to someone else. I find just enough air to cry out to the doctor again and, in an effort to help, he wraps my freezing, gnarled fingers inside the warmth of his own. I begin to sob when I realize I can't feel his hands either and look out the window to make sure I'm still alive. The breeze has stopped breathing, and the once lively leaves are now silent and still. "God is still with me though, right?!" I frantically seek reassurance from my mother-in-law. "Yes," she says as my feet start to twist on their own. I turn to look at the doctor again and as I move my head, I feel the building slide off its foundation. I grab the sides of the table and brace for impact while everyone around me stands completely still.

I feel as though I have disturbed a dormant kraken by pushing myself too far.

—KATHERINE MAY

I am digging my heels into the end of the exam table to keep from crashing through the window when I remember the bottle of Xanax in my purse. I still don't know whether I'm dying or just having a stroke, but I do know that I am very afraid, so I ask the doctor if I should take one. He is the one who prescribed it a few years back, but it hadn't occurred to him that I might carry it with me. He replies "Yes!" without hesitation, but I am too disoriented and shaky to do anything that involves a childproof bottle, so I let my purse fall open toward the nurse. A moment later, she gives me the little white tablet, followed by just enough water in a tiny paper cup. Most of its contents splash onto my shirt as I rush to pour it into my face, but for the first time in as long as I can remember, I swallow a pill and become slightly less afraid.

When I am finally back home, I go straight upstairs and sit down on my side of the bed. The room is flooded with sunshine now, but my insides are just the opposite. The small seed of fear that I have been carrying with me since I was little has now sprouted roots, and they are thickening as they reflexively constrict around the only bright spots left inside me. I slump down and surrender to a different kind of cry, and when all of the humiliation and frustration has drained out of my face, I heft my chin up and look to my top drawer. The one holding the butterfly brooch that reminds me of my grandma. I wish she was here now too. She was so good at making scary feelings go away. Most adults are, but when it comes to fear and physical discomfort, I feel like I just don't know how to do it. I want to believe it's possible, though. I want to be open to transformation. Like a caterpillar inside a chrysalis, who first goes down to liquid and then spins colorful wings in the dark.

Whew. That was such a challenging story to retell. I actually wrote it in several chunks, over a very long period of time, because revisiting those feelings in such a descriptive way often began to re-trigger them.

But here's what I want you to know, dear reader, especially if you could relate to any part of that terrifying experience: I'm okay. I was always okay. Even in the midst of torturous panic. I mean, I was afraid, for sure, but I was also okay. I was okay beneath all my irrational thoughts and frantic feelings— both of which will always come and go if we let them. It's easier said than done sometimes, but with practice, we can take the power away from all those pesky whys and what-ifs. We've got a warrior in our bones and a whole bunch of ups and downs to prove it.

One of my favorite authors, Matt Haig, once wrote, "You may feel like you are in a nightmare. Your mind might be beating you up. You may think you aren't going to make it. But remember a time you felt bad before. And think of something good that happened since, in the interim. That specific goodness may or may not happen again, but *some* goodness will. Just wait."[2]

I use that exercise whenever I lose sight of what's true, and those memories remind me that the future will always be full of fresh starts.

coming home is . . .

a spark of hope

The very least you can do in your life is figure out what you hope for. And the most you can do is live inside that hope. Not admire it from a distance but live right in it, under its roof.

—Barbara Kingsolver

I've never met a fixer-upper I didn't love. There was one that came close, though. We bought it six months before I started my blog and ten years before that scary episode at the doctor's office. It was the ugliest house on the most sought-after street—the kind of street nobody moves away from if they are lucky enough to land there. In other words, when a house pops up for sale there—even if it's slightly more than you've ever paid for a place and needs a tremendous amount of (mostly cosmetic) work—you do your best to buy it. That's what I told Kevin the day I found out it was on the market anyway. We toured the house on our lunch break that same afternoon, and although he couldn't quite see its potential, I somehow convinced him that we should try to buy it.

> I feel prettiest with sawdust in my hair and at least one bloody knuckle.
>
> —HILARIE BURTON MORGAN

On closing day, we went straight from signing papers at the attorney's office to ripping up carpet at the house—which, because of said carpet, was almost uninhabitable at the time. We bought it as a foreclosure, and the bank had clearly taken it back from a large family of cats. Or a family of large cats; I'm not sure which. But I'll never forget that stench. It set fire to your windpipe the second you stepped inside. The house had been vacant for months, but the carpet was still wet in several places. We worked as quickly as we could to remove it, but the air was so thick with the scent of ammonia, we couldn't even fully open our eyes.

Later that evening, one of Kevin's friends stopped by to help us unload our moving truck and get some of our heavier things inside. But after two trips across the living room, he asked if he could just set stuff on the porch instead. Kevin and I laughed, mostly because it was funny, but also to ward off any niggling feelings of buyer's remorse. We slept under a box fan wedged into our bedroom window that first night and woke up with litter-box breath the next day. Blech!

Putrid stench aside, that house really did give me something to sink my design teeth into, and after all the carpet was out, I felt like a kid in a 1,900-square-foot candy store. Its outdated finishes and rushed renovations were just begging for someone to fix them, and I felt so grateful for the chance to do it.

Kevin and I had desk jobs at a photography studio at the time. I helped clients decide which photos and frames they liked best, and Kevin retouched their flyaways and faces. It was fun to be creative and work with good friends, but after a few windowless years in the center office of somebody else's building, Kevin missed touring with his band, and I yearned to create a business of my own. So we did what any artsy-fartsy dreamer folks would do and quit our jobs

ME, ON MY LUNCH BREAK HOLDING MY BREATH AND MEASURING OUR SOON-TO-BE HOUSE!

so that we could both go for it. Looking back now, I can see that my departure may have also had something to do with anxiety because, although I didn't understand what had happened until many years later, I'd also had my first panic attack in that building not long before we both quit.

Working on the house was a good distraction during that season though, and when I stumbled onto something called a "blog" authored by a woman sharing about her own home-improvement projects (Hi, Rhoda!), I felt inspired to document and share our renovation adventures too. I started by signing up for a free account through Blogspot, which was the perfect price at the time because the economy crashed shortly after we moved in. Kevin's plan to go back on tour with his band came to a screeching halt, and my dream of creating an online shop with my mom swiftly went up in smoke too.

Instead, we went into scramble mode looking for work that first summer; we were so desperate to stay afloat. I responded to at least fifty job listings online, but no one answered any of my emails. Well, not until a decade later. I'm serious. I flinch every time I find a job offer from Monster in my inbox now.

One particularly dismal day, Kevin and I cobbled together a couple of résumés and brought them to a local employment agency. I remember pulling into the parking lot and being struck by how small the building was—maybe two car lengths wide by two car lengths deep? I felt claustrophobic just looking at it and took a deep breath before we slipped inside. There were two women working behind large desks that faced each other in the front half of the building, and I assumed there was a break room on the other side of the wall. The space planner in me always takes note of those kinds of things, and I wished I could help them make their environment feel better. Because when I am in that world, helping someone else come home through creativity and design, it always feels like I'm coming home to myself too.

Almost all the colors and furnishings were some shade of light brown, and I couldn't imagine what kind of toll that took on morale; it was like stepping inside a big box of fried food. I began to redesign the room in my head while the gal on our left scanned our résumés in silence.

I don't know what we were hoping she would have for us, but since neither of us had degrees and our job experience consisted mostly of fronting a touring rock band and scheduling voice-over sessions for celebrities in Hollywood (something I did before I met and married Kevin), she struggled to find a good fit for us in small-town Alabama. Especially at that time, when folks were doing more firing than hiring.

On our way back out the door, she said she'd be in touch if anything popped up. I took another big breath when we got outside and told Kevin that he probably shouldn't hold his, either.

We managed to (mostly) make ends meet through odd jobs for a while, but, thankfully, Kevin's agent was finally able to book a short tour near the end of that year, and I landed a part-time job at Michaels, where they were adamant that it was a temporary gig, just from Halloween to New Year's, but I was determined to make a good impression in hopes they would decide to keep me. I hated working the register (I was like a deer in headlights when it came to returns and exchanges. I swear I have PTSD!) but I *loved* making wreaths and stocking shelves. The repetition was relaxing and having a front row seat to all the latest and greatest art supplies and decorations gave the creative side of my mind a chance to dream.

Having steady work definitely helped lift our spirits, but when our central heat kicked the bucket mid-winter, it didn't matter how sunny it was outside, you could always see your breath inside our house.

We pressed on with DIY projects almost every day, though. They made the place look better *and* helped us stay warm. Moving my body and making low-cost, high-impact improvements brought me an enormous amount of joy during that very challenging time.

But then something totally unexpected happened on Christmas Eve that year, and the ripple effect began to change everything.

We were down to our last twenty dollars and because tensions were running high, we had just exchanged the bare minimum of words to figure out what we should eat for dinner. We both knew we could have stretched our money much further at a grocery store, but instead we decided to drown our sorrows in a sack full of small, greasy cheeseburgers from a fast-food place called Krystal. Because apparently, when you're struggling under the overwhelming weight of an impending bankruptcy, nothing sounds better than an avalanche of calories too. ⌣

Krystal was only a couple of miles from our house but, honestly, the drive couldn't have felt longer. The stress of our financial situation was really taking a toll on our ability to communicate. The silence in the car had a texture all its own, almost like there was an invisible stranger sitting on the console between us. It was an exhausting kind of quiet, and I think we both felt like we had run a marathon by the time we rolled into the drive-through and up to the speaker. After placing our order, we pulled up to the window to pay for and collect our food, but when Kevin tried to give the woman in the window our debit card, she just said, "I don't need it," and handed him our cups. We were still frozen in place and trying to make sense of what she had said when she stuck her head back out to give us our food. She went on to explain that our order had already been paid for by the driver of the car in front of us, and we looked up just in time to see the back end of a Chevy Tahoe rounding the corner and driving out of view. Neither of us recognized the car, and we had no idea who the driver was or why she had paid for our meal. The mystery of the moment had us both stuck in a trance until the cashier snapped us back to reality a moment later. "Oh yeah, and she said to tell you Merry Christmas."

Then, without skipping a beat, she thanked us for choosing Krystal and closed her little doors so she could move on to the next customer. Kevin eased his foot off the brake so our car could inch away slowly. We still couldn't believe that we didn't have to pay for our food, and we didn't want to run over anybody who might jump out to say, "Just kidding!" But no one did, and the reality of the situation finally took hold as our tires rolled back onto the main road. We clung to each other across the console, freeing tears that had been pent up for months. As we rode back home, everything that had previously come between us didn't seem to matter so much.

Sometimes, the challenges we face can feel like a trap. Like being dropped into a maze where you're forced to escape from the center. You keep trying different directions, but the longer you struggle to find a way out, the more it feels like there isn't one.

Being hemmed in on every side feels suffocating, but the *real* danger is in losing hope. So you must grab hold of it with everything you have, even when you feel like it's slipping through your fingers. Because oftentimes, the hardest thing to hold onto is the very thing that can pull you up and out.

Through that one act of unconditional love and service in the drive-through, Kevin and I found a spark of hope. It didn't fix all our problems or wash all our worries away, but it did shift our perspective. It was like getting a bird's-eye view of the maze, if only for a moment. Because it wasn't just someone paying for our meal; it was the reigniting of a tiny light and being caught off-guard enough to see it. It wasn't just free food in our bellies; that gesture was sustenance for our souls.

I didn't develop a relationship with God until later in life, but looking back, I can see how that experience models Jesus' story so beautifully. It shows how hope, service, and love are so intricately connected. One always leads to the next.

Never be afraid to trust an unknown future to a known God.

—CORRIE TEN BOOM

When we got back home, we spent the next several hours on the couch just talking, *really* talking, and our conversation was rich with optimism and insights. With each fresh idea, we could see that being the recipient of a random act of kindness wasn't the *only* thing that could make a stressful day good. So, high on the magic of the moment, we decided to put pen to paper and see how many other simple pleasures we could write down. By the time we crawled off the couch nearly three hours later, we had written almost four hundred simple-meets-significant things!

The next day, I printed our combined list onto a few sheets of white paper. Then I used my paper cutter to trim them into fortune cookie-sized slips. I stuffed them into a mason jar so we could pull one out together every morning. One of my favorites was, "Cut your sandwich on the diagonal, and eat it somewhere unexpected." They were all lighthearted and low-cost like that, and just having that one little thing to look forward to every day allowed us to extend the effects of that Krystal drive-through magic long after it happened.

I blogged about our "good jar" a few months later, and several readers said they "sure could use one" too. So the next time I was at Michaels, I invested in a case of small, hinged bale jars. I designed cute, adhesive-backed labels for the front

Whistle while you work

Hide a nice note for someone to find

Name all the colors in tonight's sunset

Cut your next sandwich on the diagonal and eat it somewhere unexpected.

of each jar, and then Kevin and I stuffed them with 365 of our day-brightening ideas.

We made them available for purchase through my blog a few days later, and when they sold out in a flash, we made more.

Now Christmas Eve always means a trip to Krystal, where we have an opportunity to become that hope for someone else. Because, yes, hope will always float, but it's our job to make it ripple.

When I'm not filling up on greasy cheeseburgers from Krystal ☺, I love to whip up one of my family's favorite recipes. My Aunt Chriss's meatloaf and my dad's skillet-fried potatoes are *so* good, I almost consider them heirlooms!

WHEN I ASKED MY MOM WHAT HER FAVORITE FAMILY RECIPE WAS, SHE ANSWERED, "CHRISS'S MEATLOAF!"

Aunt Chriss's Minnesota Meatloaf

Photo by Aubrey Sieberg

NOTE FROM AUNT CHRISS: *Paired with smashed or skillet-fried potatoes and a crisp, green salad, this meatloaf is pure comfort. It makes a pretty great sandwich the next day too!*

Ingredients:

1 lb. ground beef
1 lb. ground pork
1 tbsp. butter
1 tbsp. canola oil
1 medium onion, chopped
1 tsp. garlic, minced
¾ c. Grape Nuts cereal
1 tsp. Worcestershire sauce

2 eggs
¾ c. milk

SAUCE:
1 c. ketchup
1 c. pure maple syrup
2 tsp. dry mustard

Instructions:

1. Heat oil and butter in a 12-inch cast-iron pan; add onion and cook until translucent.

2. Add garlic and cook until fragrant, roughly 2 minutes. Do not burn.

3. Place onion mixture in a large mixing bowl and allow to cool slightly.

4. Add meat, cereal, Worcestershire, eggs, and milk to bowl, and mix just until combined. Do not over-mix.

5. Put mixture back into skillet, forming a loaf-shaped mound. Poke holes in the loaf with the end of a wooden spoon.

6. Whisk sauce ingredients to combine and pour over loaf.

7. Bake at 375 degrees for about 45 minutes, or until internal temperature reaches 160 degrees.

8. Rest for 10 minutes before serving.

Tom's Skillet-Fried Potatoes and Onions

NOTE FROM MY DAD, TOM: One night, while on a family fishing trip in Canada, I got out a cast-iron pan and made a big ol' batch of these. They were such a hit with our freshly caught fish that everyone said, "You gotta make these again!" I ended up making them every night of every trip from that one forward!

Ingredients:

1 russet potato per person
1½ sticks butter
1 white onion

Salt (to taste)
Pepper (to taste)

Instructions:

1. Slice potatoes and onions very thin. Place 1 stick of butter in a hot (seasoned) cast-iron skillet.

2. When the butter starts to foam, add potatoes and onions and stir in desired salt and pepper.

3. Keep turning the potatoes and onions over for about 20 minutes, adding in the additional ½ stick of butter along the way. Remove and serve when they are evenly golden and crusted.

coming home is . . .
surrendering to the current

Float, don't fight.
—Dr. Claire Weekes

There was a half-acre patch of wild grass in front of the old farmhouse my family lived in when I was a kid. It was tall and choked with weeds, and a few times a year the farmer who owned it would roll it all up into round bales that reminded me of giant, scratchy HoHos for horses. Every so often, the day would begin with a downpour, and the whole patch would flood, creating a big, reedy pond until it eventually dried back up.

One time, after a particularly dark and weighty storm barreled through, my brother and I found the field more waterlogged than ever. Seeing it so full ignited our imaginations, and we made a beeline out to the old, double-doored garage that sat a hundred or so feet behind our house. There, we heaved up the overhead door in hopes of finding something—anything—that would float. The garage was packed full of just about everything except cars, and we both felt like we had hit the jackpot when we discovered a dusty rubber raft upstairs. We pulled it outside and took turns blowing air through the little plastic valve, but no matter how much we tried, invisible wear-and-tear won the war against puffy and plump. You know what they say about kids and water-related adventures though: Where there's a will, there's a wave. We pulled the flimsy raft over to the pond and sloshed barefoot into the grassy, brown water. The sidewalls squeaked as we hoisted ourselves into the partially inflated boat.

> It was one of the best days of my life, a day during which I lived my life and didn't think about my life at all.
>
> —JONATHAN SAFRAN FOER

I can never remember what happened next though. Isn't that strange? That I can't recall anything about the most daring part of that day? I've always thought that was so bizarre. Nevertheless, here I sit, pounding out what I *do* remember because no matter how much fun we must have had paddling around in that bouncy swimming-pool-of-a-boat, the memory of what happened *before* we set sail has always felt like a rare and beautiful treasure too. David Nicholls wrote that "nostalgia is a useless, futile thing because it is a longing for something that is permanently lost,"[1] but I disagree. That place—the one etched in time simply because it actually happened—that place will never abandon me. It *is* me. My memories of that day may fade, but the thrill of it became a part of my tapestry, and I will always have pop-up pond water in my veins.

I believe we all have places like that. Places that feel not-separate from ourselves. Do you know what I mean? Can you think of a place so grafted into your existence that it feels less like a somewhere else and more like an expansion of yourself? A place that, for one reason or another, shaped your experience and now echoes who you are? To others, just a mark on a map. To you, a spark that has taken up residence in your soul. Sometimes, it's a childhood home you are no longer able to visit—held dear for decades and brought back to

THIS IS WHERE THE POP-UP POND WOULD POP UP!

life only in the quietest chambers of your mind. Sometimes, it's the home of a cherished family member or close friend. A place, as Pierce Brown would say, "where you find the light when all grows dark."[2] Sometimes, it's a beloved vacation destination. A "happy place" that allows you to slow down and experience nuance—all of that smaller, simpler, slower magic that feels like an interpretation of yourself.

There's a place just off the coast of Savannah that has been like a friend to me. It's called Tybee Island, and I feel connected to it whether I'm there or not. I visited for the first time in 2009 after a friendly blog reader invited us to come stay at her newly renovated vacation rental. She thought it would be fun to spread the word about her labor of love via my blog, and I couldn't think of anything I'd rather write about.

It's a six-hour drive to Tybee from where we currently live, and although the first leg of the trip consists of a stick-straight ride up I-85 in Alabama, the exit near Opelika forks onto a more scenic road that ribbons through the heart of central Georgia. For three hundred miles, the landscape rolls on like a patchwork quilt on an unmade bed, its stitches connecting very small towns to very big orchards. We can never resist stopping for homemade peach ice cream at the Farm & Market in Fort Valley—straight from the tree to the cone! And you better believe I always grab as many glass jugs of peach cider as I can carry before we get back on the road.

Eventually, we connect with I-16, which dead-ends into the old-fashioned heart of Savannah—a must-visit if you've never been. It's equal parts magnetic and shadowy, bustling and lazy, and driving downtown is dreamy because each median is lined with giant live oaks. Their long, gnarled branches, thick with ferns and Spanish Moss, create lush, sun-dappled canopies that stretch all the way over to the sidewalk. There, colorful historic homes and buildings squeeze together like old friends lined up for a picture.

On the eastern edge of town, the crisscross grid of active city streets funnels into the sole two-lane road that leads to and from Tybee. It's called Islands Expressway, but most folks know it as Route 80. At certain points, it sits almost completely flush with the marsh creeks on either side of it, and whenever we leave the mainland, I say a prayer that the weather (the moon?) won't make it impossible to get back.

Once you're across the waterway and past the friendly Welcome to Tybee Island sign, you get your first glimpse of the island's unique architecture and vegetation. Here, there, and everywhere, skyscraping cedars and longleaf pines shoot up from dense clusters of prickly pear and palmetto. Thickets of wax myrtle and cabbage palms are staples at every turn, and because the island is surrounded by wetland on the west and the Atlantic Ocean on the east, there's a magical low-country-meets-tropical vibe—a double whammy for folks like me who have a hard time choosing which ecosystem is their favorite. Crushed-seashell driveways and bike paths meet up with quirky old beach cottages with names like Clamdigger, Flip Flop, and Vitamin Sea, and old military barracks and mess halls have been converted into charming B and Bs and private residences. On the north end of the island, an enormous black-and-white-striped lighthouse has guided mariners' safe entrance into Savannah since 1736.

Tybee is only about three square miles in total, and most of the locals go way back, so word traveled quickly about the first blog post I published while we were there. I don't think we had even been there three full days when a woman named Diane invited us to extend our stay in exchange for another article about some of her rental cottages. Of course, we were more than happy to oblige and spent the next few days taking more pictures, crafting more posts, and filling up on more seafood and sunsets. The nightly fiesta of colors is spectacular between the marsh and the mainland! From golden ochre to fiery coral and blazing red to darkened plum, dusk never disappoints on Tybee. My favorite place to skywatch is on the roof at CoCo's Sunset Grille. It's nestled in the marsh on the west side of the island and has a storybook view of a marina.

ONE OF MY FAVORITE TYBEE KITCHENS!

For me, it doesn't get much better than watching colorful shrimp boats chugging back with the day's catch as the sun throws its last light up to the sky above the Lazaretto Creek.

We've visited almost every year since that first trip. Sometimes to slow down and unwind. Other times, to photograph cottages or help folks who reached out for help with redecorating. Each experience is now steeped in a myriad of warm memories.

One of my favorite experiences was sprucing up the historic Enlisted Men's Mess Hall that sits behind Officer's Row.

It was built in the 1920s, and stepping inside feels like taking a trip back in time. The kitchen may have been the heart of that home back then, but the original wrap-around porch, big old school windows, and creaky wood floors have definitely become its soul. The structure was split into two rental units at some point—one smaller (which is still called Enlisted

Men's Mess Hall) and one larger (which is now called Screened Inn) —but since they're owned by the same family, I got to dream up ideas for both sides while we were there. The budget was super tight, so I had to get *really* creative but, honestly, when it comes to make-overs, those are my favorite kind.

> Thrift is not an affair of the pocket, but an affair of character.
>
> —S. W. STRAUS

We started by cozying up the large kitchen. We pulled a sturdy farm table into the center of the room and installed a big, galvanized fixture directly above it on the ceiling. Then we added personality through pattern and pops of color. I skirted the cast-iron sink with a red-and-white-striped curtain and draped the kitchen table with a lively fabric-remnant-turned-tablecloth. Quirky signs and vintage plates added character to the Moonlight White walls, and I kept the gorgeous, original floorboards rug-free so that the first room folks walked into would be nice and easy to sweep. I brought in a mismatched collection of flowery, thrift-store china and red and white polka-dotted dishes from Target. Then I painted the backs of the open upper cabinets robin's-egg blue so every delightful piece would really stand out.

After the kitchen makeover was complete, we moved on to the bedrooms and bathrooms, following the same, easy-breezy/low-dough steps. We painted furniture here and added art and decor there. My favorite unexpected touch was the long row of white pencil starfish we suspended from short lengths of fishing line near the ceiling in the living room. Then, when we had finished the entire makeover, we held an open house so folks who had been following along via my blog could come see it in person too. Throwing open the doors on that once-in-a-lifetime project and meeting so many kindred spirits was like sunshine in my soul. But looking back on that experience, I think that may have been the last time I was able to host a group of strangers without feeling crippled by the discomfort of overwhelming anxiety. I miss it so much—that version of myself and that community. Sometimes, when I'm sitting somewhere quiet and I am loose enough to experience calm, I scan my memory for remnants of that feeling. That long-lost freedom that flowed clean, like fresh water.

Then there's Sliver Island. Like a spirited tutor, it has always spurred me toward adventure and moved me past what feels safe. Sliver Island isn't really its name, but that's what I've always called it because the part that we visit is just a long, skinny bar of sand. It's part of the nature reserve known as Little Tybee, and it is such a beautiful place to experience Mother Nature undisturbed by man. We hitch a ride with the folks from Sundial Charters, and sometimes a whole pod of dolphins will swim parallel to the boat. The tour winds through a 6,700-acre natural heritage preserve, and after navigating its maze of braided and branching estuaries, you hop off the boat and onto a little slice of heaven. One side is peaceful salt marsh, the other is reimagined daily by the unpredictability of the churning sea. But while the serenity of spending time on a desert island can be a balm for my stressed-out soul, it can also feel a little intimidating to venture out to such a place—uninhabited and surrounded by powerful water "as swervy and alive as we are," as Sandy Gingras would say.[3] But here's what I've been around long enough to truly, deeply know: Something really special can happen when you let go enough to go for it. Oftentimes, and in the words of Francesca Mariano, "You are lifted. Out of whatever pit, unbound from whatever tie, released from whatever fear."[4] Because going for it gives us a chance to reconstruct misconceptions. It can widen our world and our lives.

One time, while exploring the ocean-facing side of Sliver Island, I felt uncharacteristically brave enough to wander ahead of the rest of our tiny group. They were busy filling their pockets and pouches with sand dollars the size of their palms, and I was intrigued by a tree that had washed ashore a few hundred feet up the coast. I felt my anxiety spike a little as I wandered out of earshot and view, but I wasn't completely alone. I was accompanied by Captain Rene's ten-pound terrier, Fiddler, named after the tiny crabs that thrive in Tybee's tidal creeks and bushy coastal grasses. It wasn't the beached tree that had her headed in the same direction, though. She had spotted (or smelled) something else on the sand, and as we got closer, she quickened her pace from a curious trot to a determined gallop. When she finally reached what turned out to be a large (dead) horseshoe crab, she circled around to the other side of it and laid down on the sand. She stayed attentive in her tiny, orange life vest and kept her eyes trained on me until I closed the gap between us. It wasn't until I crouched down to get a closer look at the shell that she finally looked away, as if she knew this helmet-sized discovery would impress me and, now that I had acknowledged it, she was free to go find something else.

As she darted up into the dunes, I stood and continued walking toward the tree. The closer I got to it, the more I realized just how large and out of place it seemed on this remote band of wild grass and micro-stones. It was probably fifty feet or more in length and didn't have a lick of bark on it. Its smooth, chalky inner skin had faded from brown to silver and was mottled with intricate patterns left by the bugs who used to live there. Only the thickest parts of each branch remained, but the water must have already worked its magic on each broken-off tip because there were no longer any signs of a struggle. The tangled mass that burst from its base looked less like roots and more like a giant wall of driftwood snakes.

Photo by Billy Pope

The enormity of it unlocked an anxious thought, and I began to feel uneasy about being surrounded by so much water. Especially the kind of water that can manhandle (sand-handle?) enormous trees.

But then I looked up.

Because when life feels overwhelming at eye level, zooming out is usually the next right thing to do. The sky was ethereal blue, with clouds as thin as cobwebs strewn across it; so breathtaking I almost couldn't help but believe what I had once read about it. . . .

In the sky there are always answers and explanations for everything: every pain, every suffering, joy and confusion.

—Ishmael Beah

As I scanned it, I realized two things. One: I *hate* my anxiety. But not in a way that is helpful. Not in a way that involves enough anger to overpower it. Not in a way that fuels me with enough frustration to move in front of it. No, I mostly just hate it from underneath it. It's like an ever-filling bucket of molten lead, always pushing down and running over and dousing my ability to feel fully alive. Sure, I've gotten pretty good at distributing the weight and managing the burn, but the unrelenting cycle is exhausting, and I really wish I had the guts to break it.

Which brings me to the other thing I realized while standing there on that barely protruding slab of damp sand. Fear was making an island out of me too. Both by choice, because of how I had started to respond to it, and because that's just how fear works. It isolates you on the inside, and if you let it, it starts to isolate you on the outside too. It's like a wide, menacing tidal channel that cuts in from the sea and separates you from the mainland. It floods the base of the mountain you're made of and tricks you into believing you're no longer connected to anything (or anyone) in the deep.

You start to build excuses where there should be bridges, and when your boundaries shift and recede, you try your best to ignore the erosion.

> I look out into the water and up deep into the stars. I beg the sparkling lanterns of light to cure me of myself—my past and the kaleidoscope of mistakes, failures and wrong turns that have stacked unbearable regret upon my shoulders.
>
> —JENNIFER ELISABETH

But you don't always have to drown in a sea of your own or other people's expectations; you don't always have to thrash against the stories you tell yourself when you're afraid. You can also keep coming home with the current. You can surrender to the wind and waves and feel, firsthand, how they can surrender to you.

Things I'd Tell My 17-Year-Old Self

1 **Learn how to cook at least five of your favorite things.** If you don't do it now, you'll still be eating cereal, sandwiches, and Stouffer's when you're fifty. (I'm serious.) Join your mom or Aunt Chriss in the kitchen next time they're making any of the foods in this book so you won't miss the flavors (or the fellowship!) so much when you're older.

2 **Being grounded isn't the worst thing in the world.** When you get older, you'll actually enjoy sitting still. There's an island off the coast of Savannah, Georgia, called Tybee. From 2009 on, you will do some of your best sitting there.

3 **Weeding the garden is not going to kill you,** and this may be hard to believe, but in your thirties, you'll wish you had enough outdoor space to plant things. (Don't fret! In your forties, you will live on almost six acres, and weeding will actually feel therapeutic!)

> Weeding in good time and in loose soil is unaccountably pleasurable—steady and rhythmic, relaxing and congenially physical, leaving the mind free for reverie.
> —William Paul Winchester

4 "When it comes to solving problems, dig at [the] roots instead of just hacking at the leaves."[5]

5 **Every October, the trees all around you explode with color.** That doesn't happen in the South, where you will spend most of your adult life. As you age, you will realize that there is something incredibly comforting about the annual kaleidoscoping of leaves. Drink in your autumnal surroundings while you can, and be intentional about visiting them as often as you can in the future.

THERE IS A HISTORIC NEIGHBORHOOD IN SPRINGFIELD, ILLINOIS THAT IS PEPPERED WITH TREES WHOSE LEAVES BLAZE LEMON YELLOW COME MID-OCTOBER. THERE IS ONE IN PARTICULAR, IT STANDS NEAR THE CAMPAIGN BUGGY ON THE WEST SIDE OF S. 8TH STREET, THAT HAS LOTS OF LOW LIMBS THAT STRETCH WIDE OVER THE SIDEWALK BENEATH THEM. IT MAKES FOR THE PERFECT PLACE FOR A PICTURE!
(PS- YOU CAN TOUR ABRAHAM LINCOLN'S HOUSE ACROSS THE STREET!)

It was a good moment,
the kind you would like to press
between the pages of a book,
or hide in your sock drawer,
so you could touch it again.
—Rick Bragg

6 **Think of your life as a puzzle, in a box without a top and full of pieces that aren't yet fixed in shape.** The sky is the limit, and any picture is possible! Don't worry about the missing pieces you can't find along the way, just focus on the one in your hand and trust that it's possible to create something beautiful.

7 **"Sometimes the most important thing in a whole day is the rest we take between two deep breaths."**[6] Practice belly breathing, a technique that strengthens your diaphragm to help you breathe more easily. "Here's how to do it:

- **Lie on your back on a flat surface (or in bed) with your knees bent.** You can use a pillow under your head and your knees for support, if that's more comfortable.

- **Place one hand on your upper chest and the other on your belly, just below your rib cage.**

- **Breathe in slowly through your nose, letting the air in deeply, towards your lower belly.** The hand on your chest should remain still, while the one on your belly should rise.

- **Tighten your abdominal muscles and let them fall inward as you exhale through pursed lips.** The hand on your belly should move down to its original position.

You can also practice this sitting in a chair, with your knees bent and your shoulders, head, and neck relaxed. Practice for five to 10 minutes, several times a day if possible."[7] It will be a helpful tool when you're feeling stressed.

8 **Sleep won't always work the way it does now.** By the time you hit menopause (which typically starts between the ages of forty-five and fifty-five, and for you will officially begin at age forty-seven), you will have developed a love/hate relationship with going to bed. And *boy*, will your brain have to do some deep cleaning once panic disorder hits. Here are some things that can help:

- *You must* **make your bed every day.** It doesn't matter what time, just make sure it's made before you call it a night. Half of your nighttime restlessness will come from not being able to access sufficient covers, and you will rarely be awake enough to do anything about it during the night. Do yourself a favor and make sure they're tucked in place before you crawl underneath them.

- **Turn the thermostat down to sixty-nine degrees.** I know, I know. *Arctic.* But as it gets dark, your body begins to produce melatonin, a hormone that plays a huge role in how well you sleep. As the melatonin is produced, it sends a signal to your brain that it's time to sleep. (And the reverse is true too: As melatonin production slows down in the morning, your brain receives a signal that it's time to be awake). A cooler sleeping environment (apparently, sixty to sixty-seven degrees is optimal) promotes higher melatonin production, which encourages sleep onset and a more restful sleep. Pro tip: Your normally tense jaw will loosen at night in your forties. Hug a feather-filled pillow while you sleep. It will become habit to roll over with it resting under your chin, and that will continually save you from waking up with a sore throat.

- **As of this writing, you are still afraid of the dark, but believe me when I tell you that sleeping with any light on (incandescent or otherwise) is only going to make getting**

a good night's sleep more challenging. Here's why: Light disrupts your sleep cycles and suppresses melatonin, which can cause you to wake up more often throughout the night. And who wants to wake up and realize it's still dark? Spoiler alert: *not you.* So ditch the nightlight and get yourself some room-darkening drapes. Trust that, even if you're freaked out when you first lie down, once you drift off to sleep you won't wake up nearly as often as you do with a light on.

- **Take a shower an hour or two before you go to bed, and make sure your legs are shaved smooth with a deeply moisturizing shaving lotion.** Notice I said *lotion.* Not cream. There's a difference, and I'm telling you now so that you don't have to wait until you're in your mid-forties to experience seventh heaven. Oh, and don't use the same razor head for months on end. Replace it regularly so the blades are sharp. Also, your Aunt Chriss was right about better bath towels. Invest in the fluffiest ones you can afford and luxuriate in the way they feel as you blot (never rub) the water off your body. Then, sit down somewhere comfortable, and slather yourself with a quick-drying lotion before sliding into a pair of soft slippers. They will make for a cushier trip to bed and keep your feet clean when you kick them off and slide them under the covers. Turns out cleanliness is next to coziness too. (˘‿˘) And speaking of blankets and sheets, nice bedding helps, but what you haven't figured out yet is that comfort has less to do with thread count and more to do with how soft your *body* feels under the covers. You're welcome.

9 **Start each day by looking up. It can broaden your horizons in more ways than one.**

coming home is . . .
restorative stories

Stories set the inner life into motion, and this is particularly important where the inner life is frightened, wedged, or cornered. Story greases the hoists and pulleys . . . shows us the way out, down, or up, and for our trouble, cuts for us fine wide doors in previously blank walls, openings that lead to the dreamland, that lead to love and learning, that lead us back to our own real lives as knowing wildish women.

—Clarissa Pinkola Estés

Sanober Khan wrote that breezy days "deserve the union of two old friends,"[1] and I couldn't agree more. If you were here with me now, I would sit you down in a chair overlooking the back pasture and go get us each a glass of lemonade. Then, as we loosened to the shape of our chairs and let the sun draw out all of our muscle tension, I'd tell you one of my favorite, most restorative stories in hopes that when you left this place, it would work its magic and leave you feeling like a new woman too. "Have you heard the one about Heligan?" I'd ask. "Ooh—it's so good!" Of course, I love almost any story that involves the inside of a person's imagination and the outside of a person's comfort zone. And that's exactly what a restorative story is: It's traveling vicariously in a kindred spirit's company as they explore the road less taken. It's the striking of a match and the light that leads you home.

And as far as I'm concerned, the best restorative stories always seem to be connected to nature. Which is kind of interesting, because I've never been overly outdoorsy, what with all those stingy bugs flying around.

> I need to go outside. I wouldn't say I'm an outdoors person, but I like to go outside.
>
> —EDIE BRICKELL

But there must be an explorer somewhere underneath my irrational fears, because I come absolutely *alive* whenever I read about a person whose experience with this planet has helped them grow. Whether it's the former foster kid who walked from Nashville to Phoenix to raise awareness for the thirty thousand kids who age out of foster care every year (Jimmy Wayne) or the artsy gal who faced big new fears in a tiny old cottage on Martha's Vineyard (Susan Branch), I just can't seem to get enough of that kind of inspiration. Turns out, there's a name for our ability to use literature to improve our lives too: *bibliotherapy*. Isn't that fun to say? (Try it!) It points to the power of story and reading's effects on the brain. It has to do with the "mirror neurons" that fire in our brains both when we perform an action ourselves *and* when we see or read about that action being performed by someone else. Meaning, when people read about an experience, they display stimulation within the same neurological regions as if they had gone through that experience themselves. Fascinating, right? It's not a new concept either. Bibliotherapy has been around since the time of Plato, according to Ella Berthoud, a British bibliotherapist at The School of Life in London.

She says, "Being transported is very good for an overactive mind, and because reading a novel requires you to maintain focus for an extended period, it has a calming effect akin to meditation," adding that catharsis and healing can come through the process of identifying with a character. "When you read a great book, you live the action of the book and become the characters you are reading about, which deepens your perspective and understanding of life."[2] In other words, sometimes, in the process of getting lost in someone else's story, we are able to find ourselves.

> When we read a story, we inhabit it. The covers of the book are like a roof and four walls. What is to happen next will take place within the four walls of the story. And this is possible because the story's voice makes everything its own.
>
> —JOHN BERGER

With that said, and since we are *kind of* together in this moment, let me tell you about Heligan—the enchanted estate in Cornwall, England.

In its heyday, Heligan was the ancestral home of the Tremayne family, who lived in the manor house and tended its hundreds of acres of thoughtfully designed gardens for more than three hundred years.[3] (Think: Victorian brick walls, exotic glasshouses, flowers, fruits and veggies, lakes, lawns, and ponds as well as orchards, farmland, and a massive subtropical jungle!)

The estate was completely self-sufficient, having its own quarries, woods, farms, a brickworks—the earliest in Cornwall— a flour mill, sawmill, brewery and productive orchards and gardens. . . . By 1900 they had amassed a wonderful collection of trees and shrubs from all over the world. Follies and temples were scattered throughout and walks and rides were created. . . . It was the centre of the community.

—Millie Thom

Hard to imagine, isn't it? Not just the impressive gardens, but the idea of sharing the same passion for the same lifestyle as your great-great-great-grandparents? I don't even know where my great-great-great-grandparents *lived*, let alone what made their hearts sing. How incredible that at least one person from each of the four successive generations of Tremaynes continued to care for and celebrate the gardens all those years!

But that's not the only reason Heligan is so fascinating. What *really* drew me to the story was learning that everything but the manor house vanished at one point. (Cue mysterious music here.) It's true. When World War I began in July of 1914, Heligan's entire team of gardeners enlisted and were deployed the very next month. Before they took their leave, they signed their names on a plaster wall in the garden privy. (That's an outhouse, for those of us who have never heard the much lovelier-sounding word.) Above their names, one of the gardeners had written "Come ye not here to sleep nor to slumber."[4] Then everyone left, and in an ironic twist of fate, the gardens themselves fell asleep for almost seventy years. How, you ask? Well, sadly, most of the gardeners never returned after the war, and around that same time, the estate's last and heirless squire, Jack Tremayne, fled to Italy, saying he could no longer "live with the ghosts" of the past.[5] He said good-bye to the fan-trained melon yards, delicate tropical trees, and world-renowned camellias and rhododendrons. He walked away from the brick walls, steam-powered glasshouse heaters, and the complex and camouflaged infrastructure of rainwater gulleys. The manor house went on to serve as a convalescence hospital and later as a base for US troops during World War II. Then, in the 1970s it was sold and chopped up into rental flats. Meanwhile, unattended and lost to the brambles of time, the gardens were eventually so completely hidden that people forgot they were there.

Then, after a hurricane in January 1990, a Tremayne descendant by the name of John Willis and his newfound friend, Tim Smit, decided to explore the tangled overgrowth around Heligan. John had recently inherited the estate and was curious about what the storm had done to his family's land. They used machetes to work their way through the gnarled old forest and, after hacking their way through an almost impenetrable fortress of vines, the duo stumbled upon a mysterious wooden door set in a tall, ivy-covered brick wall.

Wild horses could not have stopped us opening that door.

—Sir Tim Smit

FOR BOTH MYSELF AND TIM SMIT, THAT LITTLE SHAFT OF LIGHT THROUGH AN OLD CREAKY DOOR GAVE LIGHT TO EXPLORING A NEW LIFE, A NEW UNIVERSE. ALL OF US NEED THAT GLIMMER OF LIGHT IN OUR LIVES, THAT LITTLE SHAFT OF HOPE.

—PHOTOGRAPHER HERBIE KNOTT

Photo by Herbie Knott

Together, they wriggled it open and found Heligan's historic glasshouses and a centuries-old flower garden in bloom. As they continued to explore, one discovery led to the next.

They found the "Thunderbox Room" where the gardeners had signed their names, the orchid and peach houses, the vineries and melon yard, and the glass-topped pineapple pit. At nearly every tangled turn, tall brick and stone walls stood beneath mountains of bramble, ivy, and laurel. Self-seeded trees had made many of the old footpaths almost impassable, but can you imagine what a thrill it was to discover so many original features and historic plants still thriving under almost seven decades of wild growth?

> In the derelict Head Gardener's Office a rusty old kettle still hung in the fireplace and in the old Paxton Glasshouse an original pair of vinery scissors remained on a nail on a wall, as if left one day by a gardener expecting to return.
>
> —LORNA TREMAYNE

Fueled by the romance of the ruins and subsequent discovery of the gardeners' handwritten farewell notes, John and Tim were inspired to bring the once-grand sanctuary back to its former glory and spent the better part of the next decade doing just that. Today, people from all over the world visit Heligan to absorb the healing power of nature.

> It was a wonderful day that will live in me forever. . . . It took me back to my childhood . . . the days of reading *The Secret Garden* and *Peter Rabbit*, I suppose. And that feeling is what actually inspired me to fall in love with it, I'm sure of it. It wasn't to do with horticulture . . . it was to do with the feeling

of finding secret places that have stories, that maybe you'd never know, but you could let your fancy run riot with it.

—Sir Tim Smit

Isn't that marvelous? Stories like those are so important to absorb when we feel disconnected from ourselves because they can spark long-lost feelings of curiosity, enthusiasm, and creativity—and when you haven't been able to access those feelings in a while, it can be a huge relief to realize they're still in you.

Take it from me. In the months following my panic attack at the doctor's office, when I was so in the dark about what was even happening, I couldn't seem to enjoy anything anymore. It was as if fear and confusion were thrust to the forefront, and anything I used to experience as good was pushed to the back burner.

During hard seasons, when we feel like our peace of mind is slipping away, restorative stories can swoop in and remind us who we truly are. With each comforting word, they can extinguish fears and reignite what's true. They allow us to step outside our current narrative and show us what's still possible.

Albert Schweitzer once wrote,

As a rule, there are in everyone all sorts of ideas, ready like tinder. But much of this tinder catches fire, or catches it successfully, only when it meets some flame or spark from outside, i.e., from some other person. Often, too, our own light goes out, and is rekindled by some experience we go through with a fellow-man. Thus we have each of us cause to think with deep gratitude of those who have lighted the flames within us. If we had before us those who have thus been a blessing to us, and could tell them how it came about, they would be amazed to learn what passed over from their life into ours.[6]

I think that goes for the experiences we have with the folks we meet in stories too. Because, somehow, simply reading about people reawakening a beloved garden halfway around the world managed to resuscitate *my* soul too. It didn't instantly change my relationship with fear, but it did help change my relationship with *myself.*

Stories are light. Light is precious in a world so dark. Begin at the beginning. Tell . . . a story. Make some light.

—KATE DICAMILLO

I discovered the story about Heligan during a particularly dark season that had me questioning whether or not I'd ever feel like my old self again. Reading it at that time was like having someone reach into my heart and flip on a forgotten light switch. It was a filling-up of "liquid rose-gold warmth," as Jeff Zentner calls it, or "whatever color is on the opposite end of the spectrum from the color of aloneness."[7] I was *inspired* by John and Tim's adventure. I was *captivated* by the description of the nearly 400-year-old place. I was *thrilled* for the centuries-old architecture and plants! The glow of those feelings proved to me that anxiety and panic hadn't completely erased who I was. I *was* still in there. At my core, I was still a curious, enthusiastic, and creative person. Like Heligan, I had just been through a storm and gotten covered up by some wild and unexpected growth. I had started to define myself by a rickety and runaway storyline, not by the true and whole story permanently sown underneath.

> She'd understood the power of stories. Their magical ability to refill the wounded part of people.
>
> —KATE MORTON

We all do that from time to time though, don't we? Give too much power to those unhelpful narratives that shrink or limit who we really are. I think that's why stories that have a connection to nature are so restorative—even for those of us who lean a little indoorsy. ☺ Mother Nature is such a good teacher when it comes to adapting to change. I love the way Jennifer Palmer, founder of Women for Wildlife, put it: "Nature shows the way forward by continuing to do what it does best: living in the moment, one moment at a time." It reminds us that we, too, are "fiercely resilient, adaptable, and full of wonder."[8] Just like the tree whose only concern is to live out the secret of its seed, our success can simply equal presence. It doesn't have to come with so many conditions, and it certainly doesn't hinge on whatever life's storms throw on top of us.

Until recently, I hadn't really thought about what kind of stories I was telling myself about myself, but it's something we all do almost all the time. Some of the stories are flexible and kind because they stem from places like passion and ambition, but others tend to be constrictive and judgmental—and those are the narratives we need to be careful with because they're usually doing more damage than we think. Self-criticism is sneaky like that. It creates for itself a nice, trusty pattern, and after a while, that (neural) pathway is completely free of speed bumps and detours and traffic jams. It's just smooth, auto-sailing from negative self-talk to something we accept about ourselves as rock-solid truth.

> Who we are and where we belong in this world are not just a function of nature or nurture. Who we are is an act of imagination. We are not just our genetic material or how we are raised. We are also the stories we tell ourselves.
>
> —JILLIAN LAUREN

We can reverse that kind of erosion, though, and the healing has to do with practicing self-compassion. Because when we encourage ourselves like we would encourage someone else, we show ourselves that we *value* ourselves. We grease the wheels of refinement no matter what our discouraging inner critic has to say.

I had a really low moment recently that involved telling myself, out loud, that I hated myself. The realization rocketed out of my mouth on a particularly humiliating day while standing beside my husband in front of the double vanity in our bathroom. If I hadn't been facing a mirror at the time, I probably wouldn't have processed it the same way (or even remembered it today), but there must have been something about seeing my wounded expression and watery eyes in that moment that allowed me to connect with myself as a "separate" person because it definitely affected my response. It was almost as though seeing my reflection gave me the opportunity to see myself for who I was in that moment: **someone going through a tough time.** And when I saw myself that way, I could feel how I was adding insult to injury. Because if any other person in my life were struggling in a similar way, the last thing I would do is tell that person that I hate them. I would immediately pull them in for a hug and tell them they're being waaaaaaay too hard on themselves. I would rapid-fire remind them what I love about them. I would assure them they're not alone and bend over backwards to prove it. To lump hate on top of hurt would just be mean and unhelpful, you know? And shouldn't we look after ourselves like we look after our friends? Shouldn't the stories we tell ourselves *about* ourselves be restorative in nature too?

I love what Dr. Julie Smith said about practicing self-compassion: "In the same way that you made time to see and hear the inner critic, let's invite the compassionate side of you to the party. The side that wants the best for you and recognizes the harm that the self-attack causes. That part of you still wants you to grow and achieve, but from a place of love rather than shame."[9]

> Dare to love yourself as if you were a rainbow with gold at both ends.
>
> —ABERJHANI

If you were here right now, I'd raise my glass of lemonade so we could cheers to not holing up in the empty spaces our oppressive storylines leave. Those narratives don't stem from a place of power. They're just in the business of convincing us to give up.

So let's pinky swear that we'll give ourselves a little relief from all the pressurized thinking going on *inside* our heads by making time to absorb (and pass on!) more of the restorative storylines happening *outside* of them. And remember, the gardens at Heligan didn't die when the weather threw dirt at them. They kept growing . . . and so can you.

Speaking of restorative stories . . .

Some books should be tasted, some devoured,
but only a few should be chewed and digested thoroughly.
— Sir Francis Bacon

Eat these books . . .

. . . if you love a good memoir

Make Something Good Today
by Erin and Ben Napier

Miracle on Voodoo Mountain
by Megan Boudreaux

No Greater Love
by Levi Benkert and Candy Chand

The Rural Diaries
by Hilarie Burton Morgan

An Invisible Thread
by Laura Schroff and Alex Tresniowski

Surprised by Motherhood
by Lisa-Jo Baker

Everything You Ever Wanted
by Jillian Lauren

The Hiding Place
by Corrie Ten Boom

Finding Freedom
by Erin French

The Ministry of Ordinary Places
by Shannan Martin

Free Country
by George Mahood

A Walk in the Woods
by Bill Bryson

A Very Small Farm
by William Paul Winchester

Hope Heals
by Jay and Katherine Wolf

The Fairy Tale Girl,
Martha's Vineyard—Isle of Dreams,
and A Fine Romance
by Susan Branch (and you must eat them in that particular order!)

Jantsen's Gift:
by Pam Cope

Little Princes
by Conor Grennan

Walk to Beautiful
by Jimmy Wayne

In my opinion, there's nothing like curling up with a good book, a sleeve of Townhouse crackers, and a bowl of savory dip. Here's the recipe for one of my absolute favorites! ⟶

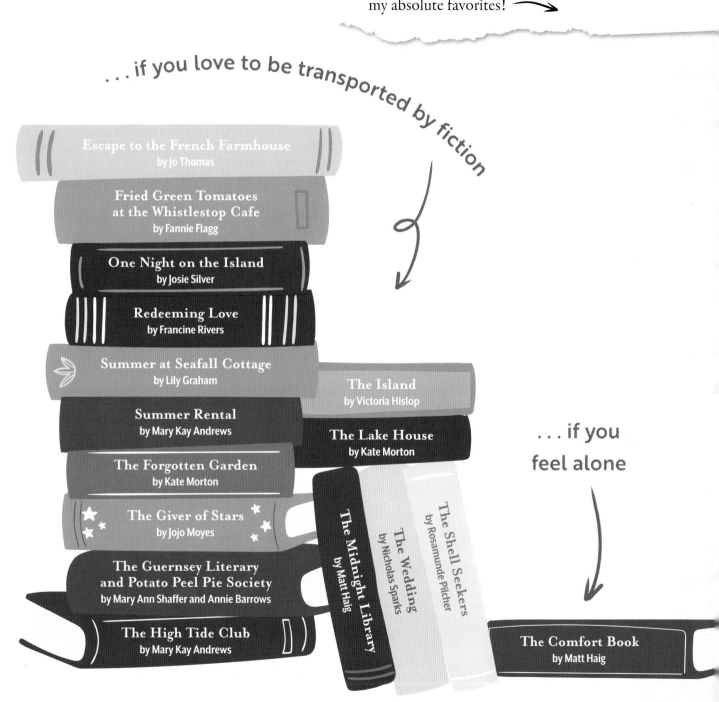

. . . if you love to be transported by fiction

Escape to the French Farmhouse
by Jo Thomas

Fried Green Tomatoes
at the Whistlestop Cafe
by Fannie Flagg

One Night on the Island
by Josie Silver

Redeeming Love
by Francine Rivers

Summer at Seafall Cottage
by Lily Graham

The Island
by Victoria Hislop

Summer Rental
by Mary Kay Andrews

The Lake House
by Kate Morton

. . . if you
feel alone

The Forgotten Garden
by Kate Morton

The Giver of Stars
by Jojo Moyes

The Guernsey Literary
and Potato Peel Pie Society
by Mary Ann Shaffer and Annie Barrows

The Midnight Library
by Matt Haig

The Wedding
by Nicholas Sparks

The Shell Seekers
by Rosamunde Pilcher

The High Tide Club
by Mary Kay Andrews

The Comfort Book
by Matt Haig

Aunt Chriss's Muffaletta Hoagie Dip

NOTE FROM AUNT CHRISS: If I'm bringing dip to a party, it's this one—my most requested dip. I always make a double batch. I fill a bowl for the buffet table and a small container to leave with the hosts (sometimes with a recipe card). I always leave some at home for us to enjoy too!

Ingredients:

½ lb. turkey, deli-style, oven-roasted, chopped

½ lb. salami, any variety, chopped

2 c. Italian blend cheese, shredded

½ c. green onion, chopped

4 pepperoncini, chopped

½ c. green olives, sliced

½ c. kalamata olives, sliced

1 c. mayo

¼ c. Zesty Italian dressing

½ tsp. crushed red pepper

½ c. to 1 c. Roma tomatoes, seeded and chopped

Instructions:

1. Whisk mayo, red pepper, and dressing together in a large bowl.

2. Add remaining ingredients (except tomatoes) and mix.

3. Refrigerate for at least an hour to overnight.

4. Add tomatoes right before serving.

5. Serve with crackers.

Additional tips from Aunt Chriss:

- Dip can also be used on buns as sandwich filling.

- The olives make the recipe quite salty; no extra salt is needed.

- Adjust the mayo/dressing amounts to make as creamy (or not) as you prefer.

5

coming home is . . .
a new chapter

Water, over time, destroyed the smooth land of northern Arizona and made it beautiful. It made the Grand Canyon. I'm sure the land was upset as it happened. Now it boasts.

The flow of your experiences, both planned and unplanned, will carve away the life you thought you'd lead. But it's busy, slowly, slowly, working.

—Jedidiah Jenkins

Every now and then, the journey we're on collides with someone who completely changes it. Their presence alters everything. It slowly, slowly smooths and expands the landscape of your life, and where there was once a mysterious mountain, there is now an extraordinary canyon.

My Grandma Evelyn and my Grandpa Richard adopted my dad in April 1956. He was three months old and nearly twenty pounds at the time. All round-cheeked and smiley-eyed, pudgy in his seemingly boneless flesh. "Wobbly as custard!" author Diana Gabaldon would say.[1] He was magnetic, and the photography studio that took his first-ever photos displayed his happy portrait in their front window for months. I think everyone knew he was the apple of my Grandma Evelyn's eye . . . until I came along anyway. ☺

My parents met and married the same year they celebrated my birth. My mom carried me a few days past her due date, and I've always been so glad I was allowed to enter the world in June. (Fellow June babies, it really is the very best month, don't you think?)

In early June the world of leaf and blade and flowers explodes, and every sunset is different.

—JOHN STEINBECK

MY DAD'S FAMOUS FIRST PHOTO—
LOOK AT THOSE SMILEY EYES!

My parents heard one of their favorite Eric Clapton songs on the way to the hospital and knew, right then and there, that I was a Layla, not a Mandy.

The three of us moved into a small apartment near my grandparents' house after I came home from the hospital, and my Grandma Evelyn and I were thick as thieves right from the start. As I grew up, our time together was always so much fun. We played games together, thrift-shopped together, baked together, and she invited me to spend the night as often as my parents would allow it. At bedtime, there was nothing better than holding my grandma's hand as I drifted off to sleep. Because while most kids are afraid of the monster under their bed, I often struggled with the one snarling inside me. I never knew what to call it at the time; nobody used the word *anxiety* back then. You were just kind of labeled (and made to feel like) a worrywart if you were troubled by an undiagnosable and uncomfortable psychological feeling. But my grandma's trusty grasp gave me safety in numbers. It helped pull me out of my head and away from whatever troubled me.

> She was my bridge. When I needed to get across, she steadied herself long enough for me to run across safely.
>
> —RENITA WEEMS

She just had this effortless way of bearing witness to my life, of folding me into her world, where all things were honest and safe and warm. I don't remember when I found out we weren't biologically related, but I do know it didn't make a bit of difference. Because she loved me beyond reason. She loved me in a way that ran so much stronger than blood, and it was the way she cared for me that really built the foundation beneath my desire to adopt.

I wasn't always certain I'd ever have the guts to build a family, though, and that uncertainty was just one of the many things I discovered I had in common with Kevin when we first met. But after twelve years flying by the seat of our pants as a just-the-two-us, and *lots* of prayer about such a HUGE decision, we finally found ourselves ready-ish (and able) to explore familyhood as we both edged closer to forty.

We started the process in December 2012. We weren't sure about all of the specifics (who? when? where? how?), but people kept promising us that as long as we kept taking one small step, we would eventually look back at an entire staircase, or in this case, *at our child*.

For us, step one (choosing an adoption agency) was the result of a series of loud and clear signs. The first one came from a longtime local blog reader named Christine. She mentioned that she and her husband had adopted their son through a local agency called Lifeline, and then that same name popped up several more times over the next few weeks. After seeing it so many times, I decided to email Christine. Within a matter of hours, a place, date, and time were set, and she had even arranged for a couple of caseworkers from Lifeline to meet with us too.

The luncheon was held at Iz Cafe in Birmingham. It's a soup/sandwich/salad place, and the desserts in the cooler near the counter are always decadent: white chocolate bread pudding, red velvet cake, mousse bombs, Oreo cheesecake—the kinds of treats you can't not try. Christine, Beth, and Iris were there when we arrived, and they were all exactly as I had imagined. Smiley and inviting, and all three of them had the kind of eyes that looked like they were lit from within. The five of us got busy pushing tables and chairs closer together, and within minutes, Kevin and I could both tell these were people we should be with. The anticipatory anxiety I showed up with wore off fairly quickly, and my nervous system regulated before we had even received our food. For the next couple of hours, Kevin and I asked as many questions and absorbed as many answers as we could. It was all so fascinating, this peek into how domestic and international adoption works; we were both totally captivated. When the time finally came to peel ourselves away, we hugged our new friends goodbye and told Beth and Iris we'd be in touch if we had any more questions. On the way home, we decided to submit an application to Lifeline, and the process suddenly seemed a little less daunting. Not a *lot* less, but a little less, for sure. I often liken it to a giant funnel. In the beginning, there's this big, wide mouth swirling with a seemingly unending number of options and questions. The funnel starts to narrow every time you make a decision or complete a step, and eventually you are matched with a child. That's when the funnel turns into a straight tube, and you pour all your energy into reaching your family at the opposite end.

A couple weeks later, Beth visited us at our home to start the home study process. She was dressed in a cozy beige sweater, dark jeans, and knee-high brown leather boots. I was wearing a considerable amount of sweat. Kevin and I sat together on our couch, and Beth perched on the front edge of our chair-and-a-half like a tiny, cheerful bird. We had an extremely territorial chihuahua named Max at the time, and most of my anxiety stemmed from hoping he wouldn't want to eat her.

Two years crawled by after that initial interview, and after countless adoption-related appointments and a seemingly unending amount of paperwork, we were unofficially matched with our son, Steevenson, in 2014.

He was two years old at the time, but we had been following his journey via Three Angels Children's Relief's Facebook page since he had arrived there six months prior. There were twelve other (mostly younger) kiddos at the Angel House orphanage at the time, and I can't tell you how many times Kevin and I visited that page—just scanning the kids' faces and wondering who our daughter was while we waited. Yeah, you read that right. Fear had me convinced that I wasn't physically fit enough to keep up with a rough-and-tumble boy, so we had only checked the "girl" box on our paperwork.

I'll never forget the day we changed our minds. (Or maybe it was more like our minds changed us?) It was May 23, 2013. I rounded the top of the stairs at our former home and saw Kevin sitting at his desk at the opposite end of the hall. I could tell his eyes were full of tears before I had even reached him, and my mind instantly jumped to the worst-case scenario. I was sure he was about to tell me someone we knew had passed away. I asked him what was wrong as I moved quickly toward our room, but when I got there, he just looked up at me and pointed at his computer. I followed his finger and saw a picture of Steevenson's angel-baby face sitting in the middle of the screen.

In an instant, and unbeknownst to us at the time, the Rockies softened into the Grand Canyon. After a few silent moments had passed, Kevin whispered, "But what if our child is a son?"

FROM KEVIN

From the second I saw his photo, Steevenson looked so familiar to me. It was as if I already knew him, or I had known him. I felt like I wanted to tell him that everything was going to be okay. Even though I wasn't exactly sure what that looked like. I felt like kids shouldn't need to worry about stuff like that, and I instantly wanted to take that feeling, that confusion, away.

> Do you know how there are moments when the world moves so slowly you can feel your bones shifting, your mind tumbling? When you think no matter what happens to you for the rest of your life you will remember every last detail of that one minute forever?
>
> —JODI PICOULT

I felt it too. An openness that I had talked myself out of before. Another step full of peace, beckoning us to proceed. We didn't know if God was guiding us *to* Steevenson, but it definitely felt like He was guiding us *through* Steevenson, and we wanted to honor that still, small voice because the message felt so calm and clear.

We called our adoption agency the next morning. I remember being so worried that they were going to think we were crazy for changing our minds about something (again), but our caseworker was actually relieved to hear that we were open to either gender and amended our paperwork that same day.

Six months later, some person, at some desk, in some building, somewhere in Haiti decided that Steevenson, Kevin, and I would make a good match, and while Kevin and I bawled together in our living room, the gentle angle of our funnel dropped off steeply into a tube.

We weren't allowed to travel to Haiti to meet Steevenson until the following year, but thanks to a little online sleuthing (Pro tip: Pay attention to who is liking and leaving comments on photos on the orphanage's Facebook page. Chances are, they're in the process of adopting too!), I was in touch with several of the adoptive parents who were a few steps ahead of us, and it was always such a gift to get their email updates about our babe.

January 31, 2014

A winter storm blew through on Tuesday. Rain turned to ice mid-morning, and our shrubs slowly leaned stiff into place with each freezing drop. By lunchtime, icy roads meant no more trips to town, so I pulled on thick pajamas and curled up on the couch with a bowl of hot soup and a sandwich filled with melted cheese. I scanned the heavens for snow from the living room window, and by late afternoon, I couldn't stop smiling as ice-cold confetti floated down from a silver-white sky. Snow doesn't happen but once every few years around here, so you'll understand why I had to pull on my boots and go outside.

I've been hearing (daily) from one of the other adoptive mamas while she's visiting her soon-to-be daughter in Haiti. She and her husband walked through the big green gates at Three Angels for the first time last Saturday, and my pulse quickens whenever I check my inbox and see that she's written. There's no telling how many times I've read and reread her updates. It's like I can't read them hard enough. Do you know what I mean? It's hard to believe I'll be jotting down the details of my own experience there very soon too. And guess what? Steevenson has our photo book!! On day 2, my friend said he carried it around "all morning long" and would climb up next to anyone sitting still so they would look through it with him. She said, "Layla, he was outlining your FACES with his FINGER and BABBLING. He is so ready for you to come and be HIS." See what I mean? *Can't. Read it. HARD ENOUGH!* Feeling incredibly grateful for the view out my window and the warmth that comes from being outlined and babbled about today.

LAYLA

We flew to Haiti four times before we were legally able to bring Steevenson home on August 19, 2016, and it seems like all those trips were just . . . how did Sharon Kay Penman put it? "Not so long ago, just a lifetime."[2]

Every now and then, someone asks me about the process of adoption, and I usually say that, for me, the experience felt very double-sided. There was both a desperation for supernatural intervention *and* a cocoon of calm. I spent nearly four years questioning every bump in the road *and* knowing with every fiber of my being that this was the path I had been called to. It was both incredibly emotionally, mentally, and physically demanding *and* indescribably rich and life-giving. Along the way, you are required to absorb countless hours of adoption-related training and education, and you are compelled to read every parenting/adoption-related book ever written. You travel hundreds of miles in order to attend seminars and workshops hosted by human development experts who

Photo by Billy Pope

are there to help soon-to-be parents understand what to expect when they're expecting to adopt. It is all incredibly eye-opening and helpful, but when it comes to being someone's mommy (adoptive or otherwise), there's really no way to fully prepare a person for an experience like that. No combination of letters could ever adequately describe the dauntless light that makes a place in your body, rerouting your blood vessels so that your heart can walk around outside of your chest. Sometimes, I put my hand on Steevenson's back and realize it's the breath in *his* lungs that makes me feel most alive.

I think that's one of the reasons my relationship with fear has frustrated me so much. When I do the things I think I cannot do, I can see that by avoiding them, I am only shrinking to a more rigid and finite version of myself. It's like clipping your wings or having seams that don't stretch. And I don't know what scares me more—the feelings that come along with being afraid, or knowing that if I insulate myself from the intensity of life, I will live a very limited one.

Take Steevenson's adoption process, for instance. If I had allowed myself to be overwhelmed by the whole staircase of adoption, I wouldn't have taken the first step. If I hadn't taken the first step, or I had allowed my social anxiety to get the best of me, I never would have had the opportunity to experience such luminous peace on the way home from Iz Cafe. If I had allowed my fear of flying to determine where I might find my family, I wouldn't know my son. And I can't imagine a life without Steevenson Chevalier Palmer. He is fresh air personified. As open as the sky and as irreplicable as a rainbow. In the words of Suzanne Finnamore, "the closest I will ever come to magic."[3]

But sometimes our insides create stumbling blocks for our outsides, and how we feel can start to affect how we act. So how do we walk the biblical encouragement to "be not afraid" when the alarm bells blaring within us tell us that we are? I love Parker Palmer's advice:

> I have had to read those words with care so as not to twist them into a discouraging counsel of perfection. "Be not afraid" does not mean we cannot *have* fear. Everyone has fear. . . . Instead, the words say **we do not need to *be* the fear we have.**
>
> We have places of fear inside of us, but we have other places as well—places with names like trust and hope and faith. We can choose to lead from one of *those* places, to stand on ground that is not riddled with the fault lines of fear, to move toward others from a place of promise instead of anxiety. As we stand in one of those places, fear may remain close at hand and our spirits may still tremble. But now we stand on ground that will support us.[4]

What an eye-opening perspective. It loosens something constrictive inside me. It rubs out the chalk line that I am always drawing down the center of myself. The one that says you can't be both fine and afraid. You have to pick a side. I started scribbling it years ago because I (mistakenly) thought it would protect me from the sensations that come along with feeling anxious. My prefrontal cortex knows that line is powder-thin and unnecessary, but my frazzled amygdala just keeps adding fresh chalk to it daily. I am thankful for the ability to compartmentalize sometimes, but I hate the way it keeps me at odds with myself and reinforces the (false) idea that fear is only there to scare me.

> Fear stands there and points you in the direction of things that are important. Don't be afraid of your fears, they're not there to scare you; they're there to let you know that something is worth it.
>
> —C. JOYBELL C.

Parker Palmer's perspective blurs the line between what *is* and what is *possible* and where there is normally a wide, dark divide, his way of looking presents to us a bridge. And that's what I want to be for Steevenson. *That's what I want to be for myself.* Because, although I am so thankful for the protective grasp of my caring Grandma's hand, I know in my heart that distraction is not the answer. By avoiding the monster who lives in my veins or underneath my bed, I might not ever know there really isn't one.

coming home is . . .
undoing the work

Sometimes the hardest part of the journey is believing you're worthy of the trip.

—Glenn Beck

Sometimes, when I'm in what psychologists would call a "low mood," which, for a person who has an issue with panic actually means a state of high anxiety, I really struggle with feeling like I'm not equipped to be a mom. I mean, I *want* to do all the normal mother/son stuff—a morning bike ride as a just-the-two-of-us while Kevin sleeps in. Two tickets to California so we can hang out with our mother/son besties, Tacy and Gregory. An afternoon play-date at Chuck E. Jesus (yes, that's what Steevenson thought it was called when he first came home from Haiti and, yes, we've all said it that way ever since—ha!) But, at this point, I've pinned *so* much fear of fear to bustling places full of busy people that jumping into those kinds of situations can be extremely challenging now. Just thinking about it makes me feel like I'm so far out of practice when it comes to being fun.

Do you ever feel like that? Maybe not because of fear, but because of some other stressor that started out as a trickle and has grown into a giant wave? A crushing tide that doesn't quite recede like it used to? One that you can no longer loosen to, even though you've been told it's possible to let it flow right through you? If so, I get it. I am acutely aware of the way nervous illness has gradually swollen in my life, and although its presence is often quite noticeable to the people around me now, its onset was imperceptible, "like an assiduous housekeeper locking up a rambling mansion, it noiselessly went about and turned off, one by one, the mind's thousand small accesses to pleasure."[1] Not all of them, but lots of them for sure. And sometimes the tug-of-war between feeling *so* excited to do life with my family *and* feeling *so* physiologically affected by anxiety makes me feel like oil and water. One part passion to one part panic; equal parts enthusiasm *and* unable to properly process emotions.

So, in an effort to baby-step my way through this blasted fear of fear, I am intentional about daily trips to CVS. It's the closest place of business to our house, and I know that going there on a regular basis will help me to surrender to Chuck E. Jesus one day too.

There's a Post-it Note stuck to the wall in my studio with my paraphrase of these words by Roy T. Bennett: "Do not let the roles you play in life make you forget who you are."[2] Maybe you need that reminder today too?

Maybe we both need to hear that, sometimes, by *un*defining some of our roles a bit, we can open ourselves up to an important kind of *re*fining too? Maybe, no matter what so many of the self-help books say, in order to strengthen our relationships with ourselves and our kids—to reclaim our life—it's not only about "doing the work," it's about *un*doing some of it too?

Because, as far as I know, there's no rule that says you must be without flaw in order to love yourself or your kids. So when that insecure voice in your head says otherwise, acknowledge it, and then move on with your day. You don't have to believe every thought that pops into your head; many of them are not true. And it's never the initial thought that undoes us—it's that we don't let go of it. Our insecurities might be in the business of turning us against our playful hearts, but I want to be the change my kids deserve to see in their world. I want to help them interpret their past and challenge their future. Shoot, I want to be the change I seek in *myself* too. And here's the good news: It's *that want* that continues to tip the scales; it's *that want* that keeps me from giving up. It's *that want* that inspires me to keep moving forward. I forget how reliable it is sometimes, when I am at rock bottom and depleted, but *that want—that genuine and unwavering eagerness to celebrate others and live fully alive*—never fully goes away, and it's important to acknowledge that. That want is like a Compass in my body. A magnetized needle standing by in some mysterious recess, always detecting and responding to strange disturbances, always helping me recalibrate after a storm. Rotating freely on a pivot, resolved to point me back home.

DO NOT LET THE ROLES YOU PLAY IN LIFE MAKE YOU FORGET THAT YOU ARE HUMAN.
—ROY T. BENNETT

We all have one. We may call it by different names, and things like anxiety, depression, stress, hormonal changes, etc., may challenge our ability to connect with it, but it's always there to "usher us along the winding paths of our life, and light up the dead points in the dim curves of our journey."[3] That want-shaped compass is always there to point us back home.

It's hard to remember when you're in the thick of it though. We're so quick to just tally things up as awful. I catch myself doing it all the time. "2018 was awful!" I'll say, because that's how my mind chooses to nutshell it. Then I'll scroll through the 2018 photo album on my phone and see lots of pictures of fun memories and smiling faces, mine included. I'll watch countless videos from that year, punctuated by the sound of my own laughter, and in revisiting them, I remember that my joy was truly genuine at those moments. I'll check the dates of said videos and find that they were often recorded within days, or even hours, of some of the things that made that "whole year" awful.

I'll give you another, more microscopic example. The other night, I swallowed part of a chocolate chip cookie before it was thoroughly chewed, and a large chunk stayed lodged in my throat for the next several minutes. I could still breathe and talk, but *man* did it distract me from watching a movie with Steevenson.

The next day, as I recounted the experience with Kevin, I caught myself ending the story by throwing my hands up in the air and saying, "And that's my life! *That* is my life."

But in saying that out loud, I also heard this truth: **Coming home is keeping a prismatic perspective. Coming home is a thorough review.** Because that isn't my *whole* life. My life is also the cookie eventually dissolving so much that, by the time Gru and the Minions meet up in San Francisco, I don't even notice the cookie anymore. My life is also forgetting that there was part of a cookie lodged in my throat at all until my husband offered me another one the next day. My life is taking him up on his offer and then pulling an *additional* cookie out of the package before I pour myself a glass of milk because (A) YUM, and (B) by showing my fear center that I am still capable of swallowing milk and cookies, I wash down another false narrative too.

But why does our mind work that way? Why does it want to wrap up so many parts of the past as "awful" when we can zoom out and clearly see that wasn't the cut-and-dried case. As Kevin said while we enjoyed our cookies that day, "It has to be *really* good before we tag it with 'awesome,' but it doesn't have to be *really* bad before we tag it with 'awful.'"

Here's why (I did a little research!): Because our brains handle positive and negative emotions in two different hemispheres.[4] Why? Because our negative emotions involve more thinking. More processing. More evaluating. More interpreting. And as the negative information churns on and on in the "unhappy hemisphere," we find stronger words to describe it (read: chapter 1). We keep trying to figure it out (aka: rumination). A positive emotion, on the other hand (or hemisphere, in this case), is processed much more quickly and efficiently.[5] We throw a quick celebration in the "happy hemisphere," then slap a big red bow on it, and voilà!—a gift we can set aside for later. No need to find any additional words to describe it because we know exactly what it is. No need to do any additional thinking about it because the emotion it inspired felt good. But when a gift like that doesn't require any extra attention, the details of its contents can start to get fuzzy. Eventually, we may even forget that it's stashed there. I guess that's why things like wonder and mindfulness and journaling and creative outlets are so helpful and important.

Those things don't prevent negative emotions from occurring, but it sure seems like that kind of "information" goes a long way in helping to distribute the weight a little more evenly, ya know? And doesn't just *knowing* that it's totally normal for us to need more time with our negative emotions help to detoxify them a bit? Psychologist Jonathan M. Adler of the Franklin W. Olin College of Engineering says: "Acknowledging the complexity of life may be an especially fruitful path to psychological well-being."[6] We may not be able to change how our experiences are processed, but we can be more careful when it comes to the language we use to describe them.

So may we all remember that (A) overprocessing *awful* is normal, and that (B) under-processing awesome is bound to happen too. The key is to slow down enough to really notice the present. (See what I did there?) ◡̈

FROM KEVIN

I think a lot of the trouble comes when we start to look at things in terms of how much progress we've made. For instance, asking "Did I overcome _____ (fill in the blank) in 2018? Did I meet a certain goal I set for the year?" If the answer is no, we might nutshell that whole year as negative. Especially if something really bad happened that made it difficult to overcome an issue or to meet the goal you had set. Trying to make progress is important, but our lives are a million moments. A collection of good and bad, and everything in between. **Progress is a _piece_ of the puzzle, not the whole thing.** And the good thing about progress is this: You can always keep making it. It might not happen as fast as you'd like, but you can always decide to keep moving in that direction.

One practical way to combat the scary things that keep us feeling stuck is to be intentional about self-care. Not the kind that looks like comfort food, a good book, or getting a mani-pedi. No, I'm talking about the kind that involves getting to know yourself better by finding ways to decompress all *throughout* your day, not just whenever you can carve out some quiet time. Because, sure, we can all find some level of comfort at the bottom of a cup of hot cocoa, but true self-care is about filling more than just your belly. It's about nourishing your *whole* self by identifying and intentionally implementing the kinds of things that will physically, mentally, and emotionally refuel you.

Self-Care Made Simple

Go Alfresco

One great way to practice self-care throughout the day is to simply head outside. It seems like such a no-brainer as I sit here and type it out, but it took me almost forty years to truly understand how impactful spending time outdoors can be for a busy brain. The great outdoors not only inspires us to take a breath and reset with a better frame of mind, it's also linked to higher levels of creativity and improved mental clarity.[7] It turns out that a "sunny disposition" is more than just a cheerful expression too. Researchers at Brigham Young University found that "mental health distress increased among the population during times of the year with reduced hours of sunlight but improved during the lightest seasons."[8] In fact, the presence of sunshine has more impact on mood than rainfall, temperature, or any other environmental factor.[9] My husband (who has a large sun tattooed on his shoulder) dreams of driving around the country in an RV when we're empty nesters, just chasing the sun wherever it's shining and letting blue skies determine where we set up camp

on any given day. Here's something else that's interesting: Studies have linked living in an area with more green space with greater life satisfaction and reduced stress.[10] And did you know that just looking at pictures of nature can spark positive activity in our brains too?[11] Yep! So if you are physically unable to go outside, make sure to spend some time looking at the world outside your window because that can have a positive effect too!

Move It

Movement is so beneficial for our bodies and minds because physical activity sends a signal to our brains to release endorphins—the chemicals responsible for feelings of happiness, calmness, and well-being. Physical activity has even been shown to stimulate the growth of new brain cells and improve neuronal health by improving the delivery of oxygen and nutrients.[12] Doesn't that just make you want to get up right now and move?! (Go ahead. I'll wait.) And did you know that walking is actually one of the many remedies for anxiety and depression? It's true. I know that for me, a simple stroll around our circular gravel drive often does wonders for my sensitized mind. (I highly recommend absorbing the sound of birdsong and the smell of earth after an afternoon rain shower too!) Here's another interesting tidbit: When it comes to working out, research shows that exercising outdoors boosts self-esteem even more than exercising indoors does,[13] so you can have fun caring for yourself well by working out in nature too!

Be Kind

I always tell Steevenson, "It's nice to be important, but it's *so* much more important to be nice" because isn't that just the truth? There's a subtle-meets-significant bit of self-care woven into that motto too, because in being kind to others,

we also improve *our own* self-confidence, self-esteem, and general well-being. Performing acts of service, sharing words of encouragement, and simply exchanging smiles with the people who cross our paths can trigger feel-good endorphins and boost serotonin in *our own* brains as well. Sometimes, when I get an especially kind message from someone on my blog or via social media, I print it out and pin it to a bulletin board in my studio. I pass by it whenever I sit down to work, and you'd be surprised how much emotional warmth a few heartfelt sentences from a stranger can generate on a tough day of wrestling with words! I call it my bucket-filler board, and I highly recommend creating one. They say kindness may actually lead to a longer life too.[14] According to medical professionals, acts of altruism cause the release of a hormone called oxytocin, which is also called the "cardioprotective" hormone because of the way it protects the heart by dilating blood vessels throughout the body.[15] How cool is that? Our own body was physiologically designed to be kind to *itself* too!

Be Mindful

Another liberating, no-cost self-care habit to get into is focusing on the present, but (and this is a big but!) it only helps if we do it **without judging how we feel or what we think about it**. I know, I know. Easier said than done, right? It's called mindfulness, and it kind of goes hand in hand with meditation. But while meditation involves the exploration of the inner workings of our mind (noticing sensations, emotions, and thoughts), mindfulness encourages us to be fully present in a moment and gently reminds us to not be overly reactive to it or overwhelmed by it. Because developing the capacity to observe ourselves and our surroundings nonjudgmentally and with compassion can have deep and nourishing effects on our well-being. In other words, being mindful helps us see ourselves and our situation in a *truer* light—not

in the false light fear can often shadow us in. "Mindfulness is simply being aware of what is happening right now without wishing it were different, enjoying the pleasant without holding on when it changes (which it will), and being with the unpleasant without fearing it will always be this way (which it won't)."[16]

Hydrate

Did you know that dehydration is the number one cause of stress in your body?[17] Yep. "In fact, it's a self-perpetuating cycle: dehydration can cause stress and stress can cause dehydration. When you're stressed, your adrenal glands produce extra cortisol, the stress hormone, and under chronic stress, your adrenal glands can become exhausted . . . resulting in lower electrolyte levels."[18] But staying hydrated will help reduce the negative psychological and physiological impacts that come along with stress. (And now you know one of the reasons I'm always lugging a large insulated cup around with me!) Turns out, treating your body to the water it needs can also improve your sleep quality, cognition, and mood.[19] Drinking half an ounce to one ounce of water for each pound you weigh is typically a great target to aim for.[20] That means, if you weigh 150 pounds, you should hydrate your body with 75–150 ounces of water throughout the day. (Pro tip: Make sure you consume it before 6 p.m. so you don't have to run to the bathroom in the middle of the night!) And speaking of bedtime, did you know that every time we exhale, we lose water weight? It's true. So after eight hours of sleep, it's super important to replenish all the water you lost overnight. Drinking a glassful right after you wake up is a great way to care for yourself first thing each morning. PS: Fruits and veggies are mostly water, so they make a great hydrating self-care snack too!

coming home is . . .
~~instant~~ old-fashioned gratification

One of the strangest things is the act of creation.

You are faced with a blank slate—a page, a canvas, a block of stone or wood, a silent musical instrument.

You then look inside yourself. You pull and tug and squeeze and fish around for slippery raw shapeless *things* that swim like fish made of cloud vapor and fill you with living clamor. You latch onto something. And you bring it forth out of your head like Zeus giving birth to Athena.

And as it comes out, it takes shape and tangible form.

It drips on the canvas, and slides through your pen, it springs forth and resonates into the musical strings, and slips along the edge of the sculptor's tool onto the surface of the wood or marble.

You have given it cohesion. You have brought forth something ordered and beautiful out of nothing.

You have glimpsed the divine.

—Vera Nazarian

It wasn't until my mom and I were sloshing around in an active waterway buzzing with much bigger boats that we had a crucial realization: No matter how fast you rotate your legs, a pedal boat on a wavy ocean will never, ever move quickly.

We were visiting Catalina Island and had rented the foam-filled, fiberglass pedalo from a vendor on shore. We're both avid readers, but we must have missed the sign warning pedal-boaters not to migrate into the wide entrance/exit lane of the marina. For several tense minutes, we were tossed around by the wakes of various watercraft ten or more times our size. High above us, flustered captains HOOOOOONKed their intimidating horns and shouted, "Get out of the way!" and "You're not supposed to be here!" at our tiny, human-powered float. At which point my mom and I pedaled faster, craning our necks skyward and mouthing our apologies to the folks trying not to plow into us with their gargantuan boats.

The year was 2003, and we were there because I had been accepted into Catalina Island's 44th annual juried art festival. I squealed when I got my acceptance letter and spent the following six months creating as many folk art paintings as I could.

> She preferred the quiet solitary atmosphere, to create in her own world of paint and colour, the thrill of anticipating how her works would turn out as she eyed the blank sheets of paper or canvas before starting her next masterpiece. How satisfying it was to mess around in paint gear, without having to worry about spills, starch or frills, that was the life!
>
> —E. A. BUCCHIANERI

Back then, e-commerce wasn't as popular as it is today, so festivals were my go-to when it came to connecting with other artists and folks who might be interested in my work. I ended up carefully squeezing almost thirty paintings into my (and Kevin's) suitcases by the time we set sail from Long Beach. My mom took the ferry over with us too, and although it was the first time she and Kevin had met, I couldn't think of a better way to introduce them. I mean, come on. An island and an art show? What a perfect combination!

The festival was a two-day event, but by some stroke of unimaginable good luck, I sold all my paintings within the first four hours of the first day, so we spent the rest of our trip sightseeing and relaxing and, well, pedaling for our lives in the marina.

MY PEDALO PARTNER

Being there among so many other artists was one of the creative highlights of my life, and selling my work to so many enthusiastic patrons so quickly still gives me goosebumps. Thinking back on it is like having electricity move through me, and sometimes, if I'm struggling with middle-of-the-night anxiety, I replay every step of that adventure in my mind to combat my intrusive thoughts. Well, minus the pedal boat one. ☺

We need our Arts to teach us how to breathe.

—RAY BRADBURY

Life got busy when we returned home to Los Angeles, and after a cross-country drive with everything I owned crammed into the back of my compact SUV, Kevin and I got married and bought a house in his home state of Alabama. Our wedding was cozy and quick. Just a handful of family and friends gathered around us in the living room of our newly purchased house.

It looked just like the one in *The Incredibles*. All low-slung, and angles, and glass. Whoever had it built was definitely a fan of Joseph Eichler. If you haven't heard of him and you're interested in architecture, be sure to look him up.

> Inspiration is an interesting thing and it can come from anywhere; a chance comment by a friend, a piece of music, or something read about in a book. Joseph Eichler's inspiration . . . came from his experience as a tenant living in a Frank Lloyd Wright-designed house called the Bazett House. . . .
>
> It was the memory of his time in this home, with its open floor plan, use of natural materials, and light filled spaces that inspired the milk and egg salesman . . . to share his love of this style of architecture by producing more than 11,000 (Eichler) homes in the Bay Area, Sacramento, and Southern California—and, incidentally, helping to create the easy indoor-outdoor style that has come to be known California modern.
>
> —MARIN MODERN TEAM

I continued to paint and sell my work for a while after the wedding, but at some point, I put down my paintbrush and didn't pick it back up for nearly two decades. *Two decades.* How does that happen? How does a person who identifies as an artist from the time they're able to talk just stop creating? How does something that brings someone a maximum amount of joy suddenly get smaller than everything else?

Honestly, I don't know the answer to those questions. But I do know this: You can pick up where you left off when it comes to creativity. And in my case, you can pick up where you left off when it comes to pencils and paint.

While I was writing this book, and in the midst of some pretty intense exposure therapy that involved intentionally moving toward panic every day, I started painting again. Because after facing my fear of physical sensations I discovered that I could count on the time spent in my studio to serve as a kind of re-stabilizer. I realized that I could rely on the gentle swoosh of a brush to wipe away many of my self-critical thoughts. I learned that, oftentimes, the eye of a storm exists in the center of a tiny bottle of acrylic paint.

> I feel that art has something to do with the achievement of stillness in the midst of chaos. A stillness which character-izes prayer, too, and the eye of the storm.
>
> —SAUL BELLOW

Twenty years ago, I used creativity to bring what was inside of me out into the world. Today, I use creativity to invite the world back inside of me.

> I had no idea how much these quiet pleasures had re-treated from my life while I was rushing around, and now I'm inviting them back in: still, rhythmic work with the hands, the kind of light concentration that allows you to dream, and the sense of a kindness done in the process.
>
> —KATHERINE MAY

So this is an invitation to consider creativity a lifeline when you're in over your head and having trouble catching your breath. And don't worry if painting isn't your thing. Creativity looks different for everyone. It doesn't always mean designing something tangible with your hands. For some folks, creativity means working with words or crafting a memorable experience. Organizers calm frazzled nerves by creating order in our closets, while musicians transport us to other places with their melodies. There's a man in Rhode Island who creates "becorns" out of acorns that thrill our hearts and expand our appreciation of nature.

For others, "the tools at hand might be needles and thread; or a jeweller's torch; or a rack of cooking spices; or the time to shape a young child's day," Terri Windling writes.[1] Creativity is really anything that makes you excited; it's something you want to learn. It's when you "wish that something might exist, and then you work on it until it does," as Wim Wenders put it.[2]

There is creativity in all of us. In fact, an important research study showed that 98 percent of us are extremely creative right from the start, and that we only gradually lose that flame over time if we're not intentional about fanning it. Here's how we know:

In 1968, NASA hired Dr. George Land and Beth Jarman to develop a creativity test that measured divergent thinking—the ability to look at a problem and propose multiple solutions, or to look at a particular object and come up with multiple ways to use it. (Take a wicker basket for example. It could be something to store things in, wall decor, a pendant light shade—you get the idea.) NASA then used the test results to determine which potential scientists and engineers were the most open and explorative. In other words, which engineers were the most creative. The success of that experiment sparked a lot of questions and inspired Dr. Land to conduct the same research study on a group of 1,600 four- and five-year-old kids. The results were astonishing. Get this: 98 percent of the children in that group fell into the **genius** category of imagination! But when the same group of kids took the same creativity test five years later (when the kids were ten) only 30 percent of them qualified as creative geniuses. Then, when he tested the same kids again at age fifteen, that number dropped to 12 percent. But that's not all, and you may want to sit down for this next bit: When 280,000 *adults* were given the same test, the number of creative geniuses dropped to 2 percent.[3]

PERCENTAGE OF PEOPLE WHO QUALIFY AS A CREATIVE GENIUS:

At 5 years old	98%
At 10 years old	30%
At 15 years old	12%
Adults	2%

The researchers concluded that non-creative behavior is learned.[4] Or, as one writer put it, "All children are naturally creative. Our job is not to cultivate their creativity, but to refrain from crushing it."[5]

Isn't that such an incredibly powerful insight? I felt more equipped just having read it. It makes sense that non-creativity would be a byproduct of stay-in-your-lane thinking, though. I mean, how much higher would that last percentage be if, when they were children, more of those grown-ups had been given the freedom to invent, and explore, and tinker with things? To color the grass anything other than green?

I read a story along those lines just today, written by a man named August Turak. He had a creativity-related epiphany that really enlightened me.

In the early 1980s I was trundling along on a New York subway with a colleague when he suddenly said, "14, 18, 23, 28, 34. What is the next number in this series?"

For the next ten minutes I manfully tried to figure out the mathematical relationship among these numbers. Finally, as we stepped off the subway I admitted I was stumped. My colleague, with a devilish grin, merely pointed at the 42 emblazoned on the wall of the subway station. We had just traveled from 14th to 42nd Street, and it had never occurred to me that the answer was a stop on the subway. I had been so locked into the assumption that numerical problems had mathematical solutions that I failed to notice the answer staring at me from the pillars of every station.[6]

So for us grown-ups, creativity is actually a kind of *un*-learning then, isn't it? It's a loosening to the exhilarating and ever-changing experience of seeing where something goes. It's letting curiosity take the reins and readjusting the lens that the world keeps pulling out of focus.

> The mind is not a vessel to be filled, but a fire to be kindled.
>
> —PLUTARCH

Creativity is so important when it comes to our mental health. Especially now. With so much *ta-da*! right at our fingertips, it's becoming way too easy to just sit back and do the opposite. But what if coming home means consuming less and creating more? What if coming home is *old-fashioned* gratification?

FROM KEVIN

When we look at who we are, where we came from, how we got here—it's all creativity. I can get really lost in that. I mean, I'm part of a complex creation, I _am_ a complex creation, and I can turn nothing into something with _my_ mind too. That's powerful stuff.

Sometimes, I spend too much time in my head in the opposite way. I question my worth and wrestle with a lot of self-doubt. I move in on myself too harshly and, in turn, pull away from who I truly am. That's when I know I need to dive into a creative project. Because writing lyrics or chasing melodies always brings me back home. And when I'm in that place—where I'm not judging myself, and I can actually forget about the thoughts that are closing in on me—it's like stepping into an alternate universe. Into my truest self. Creativity is another dimension that allows you to get into it.

It doesn't always work like a light switch for me. There's usually a hump to get over first. But when I do, I lose track of time. I tap into something bigger than myself.

As Zig Ziglar wrote, "People often say motivation doesn't last. Neither does bathing—that's why we recommend it daily."[7] I think the same goes for creativity. You have to keep coming back to it. Because the longer you're away from it, the more time you have to construct a story about the world and your life that isn't necessarily true. Creativity recalibrates. The world doesn't feel so scary after I play my guitar. Because I believe in what's possible. Because I just felt it.

coming home is . . .

an invitation

*Should your spark start to fade
because of stress or time or fear,
you'll need reminding of your flying
and the reasons we are here.*

*To fly and help each other fly—
it's wild and it's true.
To fly and help each other fly
is what we're here to do.*

—Brad Montague,
Becoming Better Grownups

I t's sweet how some things just feel like February. Boxed chocolates, red hearts . . . our very own Katie Sue. My mother-in-law was born a few days after Valentine's Day in 1936 and turned eighty-three years young shortly after we all moved in together in 2018.

Five years later, she's still an active gal, and her desire to serve remains as important and natural to her as breathing. Most days, she races off right after breakfast. Sometimes to rehearse with the Joy Singers at church, other times to bring food to folks who are sick or grieving. Sometimes, she has an appointment with a doctor or a dentist, or with Mrs. Pinkston who takes care of her hair.

She rarely misses the once-a-month luncheon for State Board of Missions retirees, where she fills up on food that comforts and fellowship that does too. Every Thursday morning, she helps label *The Beacon*, a tri-fold publication that's mailed out weekly to First Baptist's entire congregation. I once asked her if she reads it while she labels them and she said, "Oh, no, I like to wait until it comes to the house." I smile every time I see one in our mailbox now, knowing it was sent *by* her, *to* her, and that it will *still* feel like a surprise.

When Katie isn't out and about or buzzing around her kitchen preparing meals for herself and Kevin's disabled dad, Jim, we can usually find her in her chair. It's a big, puffy, cloud of a thing, and if you're even the *teeniest* bit tired, it will snuggle you right to sleep. The day Katie and I went to look at the chair, we were both solely focused on things like color, and price, and how we would get it home. But now that it's been here a while, that chair is so much more than just batting and fabric stapled to wooden bones. Now it tells a story of the person who sits in it—our beloved Granmé Katie, as our family calls her now, who stays as busy in it as she does out of it.

> Every choice to slow down and attend to what *is* with our whole selves is an invitation to belong more fully and engage more deeply with this life we've been given.
>
> —SHANNAN MARTIN

If it's too dark to be out driving, she checks in on folks from her chair. Armed with a cell phone and a sunny disposition, she kicks up her feet and punches in numbers, not letters, genuinely hoping that the person those digits belong to will pick up. Her conversations are as comfortable and soft as the seat beneath her, her cheek as hot as the sun by the time she's done.

Some days, Katie uses the chair to serve people in a totally different way. Armed with a needle and thread, she creates the small, evenly spaced gathers of a pleated yoke before passing it on to the next member of the Jackie Swan Missionary sewing team. Like candles lighting candles, they work together, piece by precious piece, to create smocked burial gowns for the stillborn babies whose souls shine on in heaven.

Other times, she is awake and quiet in her chair; the only sound we hear is the patient turning of pages. We know what she's reading. Her favorite Book. The story that ends around page 1,200 in her hands but goes on forever in her heart. The story inspired by the Author who loves her and loves others through her—right there from her chair.

Sometimes, instead of "swimming upstream in a world that . . . chooses practicality over poetry,"[1] Katie makes time to write things down.

Abundant Grace

BY KATIE PALMER

When the lightning flashes
And the thunder rolls
Our Lord and Savior
Is still in control

The storm clouds gather
And cause us fear
But God has promised
He is always near

If we stop and listen
For God's still voice
He will help us
Make the right choice

No matter what trials
We may face
God always gives us
His abundant grace

One of the things I love most about Katie is her passion for cooking and her ability to make leftovers last. Nothing goes to waste in her kitchen. I bet she could stretch an Easter ham all the way to Thanksgiving! But in July of 2014, while reaching into her refrigerator to pull out the previous day's fixin's, she suddenly felt something strange bolt throughout her upper body. Almost like an electromagnetic pulse or something akin to lightning. Startled, she quickly abandoned the dish and sat down at the kitchen table.

A week or so later, a scan of her brain revealed two non-cancerous tumors—one on each side of her head. She said she had a "real, good cry" after her doctor broke the scary news, but by the time she called to tell me and Kevin, she was as calm as a millpond. Sure, she tripped over the word "meningioma" a couple of times before it finally came out right, but we both knew what she meant. We both knew it wasn't a good thing, times two.

> When things fall apart, the broken pieces allow all sorts of things to enter, and one of them is the presence of God.
>
> —SHAUNA NIEQUIST

She told us the larger tumor needed to be removed right away, and what that meant in terms of preparation and brain surgery. She told us that her doctor said this procedure had a high success rate and that she had replied, "Well, that's good because I plan on living to be one hundred." Then, for the most part, she went back to business as usual.

Because of my proclivity to panic, I was in awe of her ability to pick up where she left off. I couldn't imagine coping with the kind of stress that comes along with an operation that divides one's life so markedly. But she just kept plugging away. Always making time for other people and whipping things up in her kitchen.

> The routines you are able to maintain during a crisis are the ropes you will use to pull yourself through, back to yourself.
>
> —DR. JENN HARDY

There are times in your life when you can feel that things are about to change in a big way. You don't know exactly how, but you notice the axial tilt of your world has shifted ever so slightly. When we hung up the phone after talking to Katie, Kevin and I knew this was one of those times. Questions flooded our minds: What if there were complications? How would Katie get around if she needed to go somewhere? With Katie out of commission for a while, who would take care of Jim? What if another health emergency popped up? The more questions we asked, the more one answer became clear: We would create a comfortable addition on the south side of our house so we could all do life together. **Because sometimes, coming home is someone else coming in.** Sometimes, coming home is opening the door, or in this case, creating a new one.

A week before Katie's surgery, we met up with two of her sisters at Peyton's Place, where the four of us all chose the meat-and-three with a side of cornbread. It was one of my favorite lunches of all time. Not because of the food (although I highly recommend the baked tilapia, rice and gravy, green beans, and banana pudding), but because there's really

LUDIE, SHIRLEY AND KATIE

nothing like the company of three senior sisters sharing childhood memories and grown-up dreams. After that, we all drove down to Eastbrook Flea Market, and when we were done combing nearly all sixty thousand square feet of glorious secondhand stuff, we wandered next door so Katie could try on wigs.

A week later, the operation went smoothly, and Katie went on to recover in record time. Proving, once again, that tough situations can, in fact, build even tougher people.

We've been under the same roof for nearly half a decade now, and although we don't always get our reactions right, I know we're all committed to trying. Not because we're perfect, but because we keep choosing to believe that our imperfections are "arranged in a way" that allows us to "hinge together," as author Lisa Kleypas would say.[2]

> What unites us is the mutual resolve to hold one another in kind regard, learn the histories parceled out as trust grows, imagine the complexities, anticipate the hurdles, and notice the joys each of us carries.
>
> —SHANNAN MARTIN

And when I think about the invisible tether between us now, I see a sturdy, covered bridge that shelters us all. One that is held in place by the investment of time and that is constructed out of our shared desire to care for each other. Under its roof, we hold space for one another; we sit together when we are unable to stand on our own.

We're all designed to connect that way; we're all here for love and service. It doesn't always look the same for everyone, it doesn't always mean moving someone into your house. It just means inviting people into your *life*. It's a purpose-driven call to be open. It's allowing your triumphs and your pain to inspire and minister to others. And, in turn, allowing them to inspire and minister to you. Because, yes, coming home *is* about finding yourself but sometimes, opening up and allowing others in is *how* you find yourself.

Katie's Lemon Icebox Meringue Pie

NOTE FROM MY BROTHER-IN-LAW, KERRY: *One of my fondest childhood memories is watching my mother make this lemon icebox pie. Each time she made one, I would stand in the kitchen and visit with her throughout the process. When I was a teenager, I asked if I could learn how to make this delicious dessert for myself. I still use her handwritten recipe every time I get to work on another pie for a family get-together. Her handwriting on that battered old card is very special to me, and I still choose to keep it in front of me even though I don't really need it. You see, that simple pie (while it tastes very, very good!) is all about love and memories of a very happy childhood.*

Ingredients:

14-oz. can Eagle brand sweetened condensed milk (may use fat-free milk if desired)

2 eggs, separated

½ c. lemon juice

4 tbsp. sugar

FOR CRUST (RECIPE COURTESY OF AUNT CHRISS):

1½ cups graham cracker crumbs—regular or cinnamon

3 tbsp. sugar

⅓ c. butter, melted

Instructions:

1. Stir together graham cracker crumbs, sugar, and butter; press into pie plate.

2. Bake at 350 degrees for 10 minutes or until light brown. Let cool.

3. Place milk in mixing bowl.

4. Separate eggs and place the yolks in milk. Place whites in separate mixing bowl.

5. Add lemon juice to milk and yolks. Blend well until mixture thickens.

6. Pour mixture into store bought or homemade pie shell.

7. Beat egg whites with an electric mixer until peaks begin to form.

8. Add sugar and continue to beat until mixture stiffens into meringue.

9. Cover pie with meringue and bake at 350 degrees for 15 minutes, or until golden brown.

10. Cool slightly on a wire rack, and chill until firm before serving.

Katie's Key Lime Cake

NOTE FROM KATIE: I shared the stacked version here, but you can also bake it for 32-35 minutes in a 9x13 pan.

Ingredients:

CAKE:
1 box lemon cake mix
1   3 oz. box lime Jell-O
⅓ c. vegetable oil
3 eggs
½ c. orange juice
¾ c. water

GLAZE:
1 lb. box confectioners' sugar, divided
¼ c. key lime juice (bottled)
¼ c. key lime juice (fresh)

FROSTING:
1 stick margarine (softened)
8 oz. cream cheese (softened)
1 tsp. vanilla flavoring

Instructions:

1. Prepare 3 round 9" pans by lining the bottom of each with a 9" circle of waxed or parchment paper.

2. Grease the waxed paper with cooking spray and sprinkle with flour.

3. Mix the cake mix, lime Jell-O, oil, eggs, orange juice, and water together for 2 to 3 minutes at medium speed.

4. Pour an equal amount of the batter into each of the lined cake pans.

5. Bake at 350 degrees for 25 minutes.

6. While the cakes are baking, knead two key limes against a hard surface to loosen the juice inside of them.

7. Cut each lime in half.

8. Squeeze ¼ cup of fresh key lime juice into a small bowl.

9. Pour ¼ cup of bottled lime juice into the bowl of fresh lime juice.

10. Mix in 4 tbsp. of confectioners' sugar.

11. When cakes come out of the oven and are still warm, use a spoon to drizzle the glaze mixture onto the entire surface of each cake before removing from the pans.

12. Cream the margarine and cream cheese together.

13. Mix in the remaining confectioners' sugar and vanilla. Mix until frosting is smooth.

14. Remove first cake from pan, discard waxed paper, and spread a layer of frosting on top.

15. Remove and stack second cake (discarding waxed paper) on top of the first and spread a layer of frosting on the top.

16. Remove and stack third cake (discarding waxed paper) on top of the second and spread a layer of frosting on top. Use remaining frosting to cover the sides of the cake.

17. Place the cake in the refrigerator to keep the frosting firm.

Dessert is like a feel-good song and the best ones make you dance.
— Edward Lee

Our Family's Favorite Spaghetti

NOTE FROM KEVIN: *I've never been a big "pasta guy," but boy have I always loved my mom's spaghetti. I didn't realize how lucky I was until I went to a friend's house when I was in fifth grade, and they served me plain noodles with sauce on top. I spent the rest of the night explaining how great my mom's spaghetti was—ha!*

Ingredients:

4⅓ c. water
1 envelope dry Lipton onion soup
8 oz. package of spaghetti
1 lb. ground chuck or turkey
garlic salt to taste
2 tsp. oregano
1 tsp. basil
2–14.5 oz. cans diced tomatoes

Instructions:

1. Bring water with onion soup to a boil.

2. Add spaghetti and cook uncovered for 15 minutes.

3. Do not drain spaghetti.

4. Brown meat, drain, and return to skillet.

5. Sprinkle with garlic salt and add oregano and basil.

6. Purée tomatoes in blender and add to meat mixture.

7. Simmer for about 30 minutes.

8. Add meat sauce to spaghetti and mix well.

9

coming home is . . .
remembering who you are

There was rarely an obvious branching point in a person's life. People change slowly, over time. You didn't take one step, then find yourself in a completely new location. You first took a little step off the path to avoid some rocks. For a while, you walked alongside the path, but then you wandered out a little way to step on softer soil. Then you stopped paying attention as you drifted farther and farther away. Finally, you found yourself in the wrong city, wondering why the signs on the roadway hadn't led you better.

—Brandon Sanderson

Every November, I am struck by the overwhelming urge to open a Christmas shop. It happens as soon as I start decorating and wrapping presents, because that's when I discover what kind of paper or ribbon or ornament is missing from the marketplace, and I am *certain* wild horses will not stop me from launching a whole line by the same time the next year.

And if money were no object, ooh-wee! I'd *really* go nuts. I'm talkin' *Full. On. Christmas. EXPERIENCE.* The one that exists in my imagination is so dreamy. Let me give you a tour.

. . . Picture a wooden barn, washed in faded red paint and accented with a winter white *X* on every Dutch-style door. Each window is trimmed with fresh evergreen swags and frosted with glittering snow. Inside, the atmosphere is lively and warm. Dean Martin is singing "A Marshmallow World," and the air smells of pine and peppermint. It's the kind of place that makes you feel like a kid again. There's a wall full of vintage Christmas ornaments: Shiny Brites, dioramas, and winking Santas, just to name a few. There are old-fashioned tree skirts and stockings made from antique quilts and winsome bottle brush trees in every size and color. Upstairs, the entire hayloft is devoted to Department 56. Thirsty? No problem. We've got thick-handled mason jars full of apple cider, freshly simmered with butter, brown sugar, cinnamon, nutmeg, allspice and just a pinch of salt. Hungry? We've got ya covered there too. The back half of the barn has been converted into a café (the warm pimento cheese sandwich and creamy basil soup are my favorites!), and there's a dedicated dessert area too. It's teeming with colorful cookie tins and tiered stands stacked high with homemade treats. Think spicy pumpkin fudge, eggnog creams, pistachio cranberry bark, peanut butter snowballs, peppermint meringues, gingerbread marshmallows and more! Out back are fuzzy animals to pet and feed, and an old Chevy pickup with a bed full of fluffy evergreen wreaths, still dewy from this morning.

Dreamy, right? It always feels so doable on a good day. In my heart of hearts, I feel like that atmosphere would be right up my alley. But then I step back and think about how unpredictable my anxiety is, and how challenging it is to not let it get the best of me, and I start to believe the voice that tells me I won't ever be able to do it.

Is there something like that in your life? Something that feels like a tug-of-war between *so* imperative and also *so* impossible?

One thing that has helped me with that particular battle is practice. That may sound super obvious, but let me ask you this: When it comes to practicing the thing that feels *so* imperative and *so* impossible in your life, are you actually doing it? Like, on a consistent basis? Take my dream/dilemma for example. I need to ask myself: Am I actually practicing, on a regular basis, to become the kind of person who would create a Christmas shop? Or am I just letting *impossible* dictate my days and never actually handing *imperative* the reins? Am I *ever* moving in the direction of my dream? Or mostly just giving in to my dilemma?

And what does that look like in practical terms? Or as Kevin would say, "What does that look like on a Tuesday morning?" Well, in this case, and as I've mentioned in different ways from the very beginning of this book, practice looks like replacing avoidance with action. It looks like feeling scared and then remembering you are brave. It's doing something that helps you remember who you are and Whose you are. Practice is intentionally proving that the person you want to be is the person you truly are.

> **Practice is imperative taking impossible by the hand and saying, "I'm not calling you that anymore."**

In other words, practice is not pitting imperative and impossible against each other, which most of us are so prone to do. It's *allowing* the imperative to make the impossible *possible* by gently and consistently re-shifting your mindset.

I'll give you an example: The other day, Kevin and I found ourselves waiting in a very tight and slow-moving checkout line at the supermarket. It made me feel sweaty and trapped, and the longer we waited, the more I just wanted to abandon the groceries in our basket. But then I remembered what I shared with you in the previous paragraph, and with that slight shift in perspective, I was able to see that standing there squirming wasn't *only* an uncomfortable experience; it was *also* an opportunity to practice doing life while feeling anxious. Because by going through with the transaction, I wasn't just facing a fear, I was also getting my favorite yogurt (key lime with white chocolate chips and graham cracker crumbles!). And when it comes to overcoming irrational fear, there's no other way to do it. You have to loosen to it to move through it.

> Practice is the hardest part of learning, and training is the essence of transformation.
>
> —ANN VOSKAMP

And remember, victory isn't based on how you feel while you're practicing. Victory is simply showing up and trying. Because feelings aren't fixed, and actions are facts. And take it from me, as intimidating as practicing can be, even the smallest of victories can impact you in a big way. Because when you push *those* kinds of boundaries, you get to see yourself again. You are coming home to who you truly are.

coming home is . . .
rewriting the story

Trouble is a tunnel through which we pass and not a brick wall against which we must break our head.

—Chinese proverb as quoted by Dr. Claire Weekes

I love a road trip. That hasn't always been the case (as I mentioned in the beginning of this book!), but lately they've felt a lot like therapy. Maybe even *better* than the traditional talking kind. I mean, they both allow you to pause and reflect on your everyday life, but I love the way an adventure can snap you out of your routine because you physically remove yourself from the center of it. Exploring not only broadens your view of the world, it also gives you a chance to "sound the depths" of your being.[1]

Travel is the great leveler, the great teacher. . . . A long stretch of road will teach you more about yourself than a hundred years of quiet introspection.

—PATRICK ROTHFUSS

And I'm not just talking about a plan-it-in-advance kind of road trip. I mean anything out of the ordinary that can create *actual* room for growth and change. Any journey that will give you some time and space to see your situation with fresh eyes. Anything that will allow you to get outside the circumstances that are preventing you from connecting deeply with yourself and that are causing an elevated level of stress.

I mentioned that travel hasn't always felt like therapy to me, though, and I feel I should expand on that a bit because something extremely helpful happened while I was far from home one time, and I've wanted to tell every anxious person about it ever since.

Something I've really struggled with along the way is unexpected physical symptoms and sensations. That two-week little spasm in my temple *(sign of an impending stroke?)*, that pop-up piercing pain in my calf *(surely it's a blood clot!)*, that cluster of red vessels on my eye *(is it going to explode?)*. For whatever reason, my immediate response to anything out of the ordinary health-wise is to stop, drop, and overanalyze. I *need* to know what is wrong with me and how to make it go away fast. For years, I frantically searched for answers in books and in bloodwork, and when I couldn't find peace of mind there, I'd change other aspects of my life. I would alter the way I ate *(wouldn't want to choke!)*, stop doing things I liked to do *(what if my eye explodes while I'm out antiquing alone?!)*, and I'd stay as close to my safe person as possible *(Kevin is the only way to stay calm.)*. I obsessively scanned my surroundings and myself. If there were an award for checking one's pulse, I would have won it in 2010. I controlled my environment at all costs to prevent myself from feeling afraid. But here's what I know now that I wasn't open enough to understand back then: In actively preventing myself from *feeling*, I was actively preventing myself from fully *living* too.

It wasn't until 2015 that I started to understand what the heck was happening to me and why none of that hypervigilance was ever going to help. And I kid you not, I ended up finding that clarity on a road trip. One that I didn't even want to take because *"There are so many miles between hospitals and what if I need one?"*

It all started when Kevin and I were invited to meet up with his former worship team in Texas for a two-night event at The Mission Church in Mount Pleasant. I was going through another extra-anxious season at the time because of some health issues I was dealing with, but we hadn't traveled anywhere in a while, and I could tell Kevin *really* wanted to go. Heck, *I* really wanted to *want* to go. I used to love to jump in the car just to see what was happening across some state line! I once filled up my extremely fuel-efficient car and drove so many consecutive miles that by the time I did need to stop for gas, I had to pump the brakes several times just to flush out the air and get the car to slow down. Ah, the good ol' days. ☺

I went back and forth on whether or not to go to Texas for several weeks, but in the end, I decided to go for it, in hopes that it wouldn't be as challenging as I was afraid it would be and to give Kevin a chance to do what he loves most—sing and play music with and for other people.

The Mission Church is downtown on 3rd Street in a historic building that used to be a movie theater when it was built in 1913. Back then, it was the only cinema between western Arkansas and Dallas, and the old box office and window are still a part of its historic facade today. I remember being *so* nervous when we first pulled up, what with all the unknowns waiting inside, but it wasn't long before the building's original architectural details had inspired me to grab my DSLR camera and explore. I must have taken a hundred pictures of that old place while Kevin and the band rehearsed, and eventually I felt comfortable enough to walk toward the town center, which was a few blocks away. When I spotted the coffee shop at the corner of Jefferson, I just had to see what was inside. Well, I just had to *smell* what was inside. I'm not a coffee drinker anymore, but I still looooove that nutty-meets-caramelized aroma. I've actually considered investing in a coffeemaker just so we can use it as an air freshener in our house—ha!

The coffee shop was called Jo's, and it was located in a historic, two-story brick building that had a giant, freshly-repainted Dr. Pepper advertisement on one side—one of those old-timey ones that makes you think, *I wish companies still advertised that way!*

After snapping an artsy photo of the azaleas out front, I pulled open the door and found the loveliest high-ceilinged cafe inside. It was clear straight away that whoever decorated the place loved antiques as much as I did. Old, Victorian-style sofas and vintage granny-chic armchairs were gathered together in groups to create cozy seating areas for reading, writing, chatting, and coffee. Secondhand end tables, quirky old table lamps, and stacks of vintage books rounded out each inviting arrangement. Vintage jars filled with fresh flowers were the perfect finishing touch atop farmhouse tables surrounded by mismatched wooden chairs. The barista counter was in the middle of the building, and beyond that was a place for local musicians to play. A low, walnut-stained wooden platform topped with an eight-by-ten rug made for the perfect casual stage, and a cluster of vintage trunks and suitcases, along with industrial-style stools and spotlights, added just the right amount of edge. The woman who owned the shop came through the back door as I was snapping a photo of the stage, and you can imagine how surprised I was when she revealed that she followed me on Instagram! We spent the next hour chatting about decorating, and the building, and anxiety, and taking leaps of faith, and let's just say, I left feeling beyond inspired to start a small business as I floated back out the front door.

Kevin was shocked when I showed up at The Mission Church, talking a mile a minute about where I had been. It was just so unexpected, especially after he'd seen me struggle with so much panic and anxiety throughout our twelve hours together on the road. He heard more about the coffee shop and my desire to create a Christmas barn on the way back to our hotel.

> Little victories are everything in a world where worst-case scenarios are on an endless loop in your head.
>
> —SARA BARNARD

Later that night I saw a quote that read, "If you are feeling helpless, help someone," attributed to Aung San Suu Kyi, and thinking back on my time at the coffee shop, I couldn't help but notice how, by swapping one word, that concept could apply to feeling disconnected from yourself and others too. I whispered the alternate version from beneath the covers of our hotel bed: ***If you are feeling disconnected, connect with*** *someone.* Sometimes, that's easier said than done, but boy, can it be a path to transcendence.

The next day, I felt even more invigorated. So after a quick continental breakfast, I dropped Kevin off at the church and set off to search for a beautiful state park I had read about on someone's blog. Unfortunately, I never did find the park, but *man*, did I feel reconnected to the adventurous part of myself! Seeing that area in person and exploring it on my own was like opening the lid of a treasure chest. Except not from the outside. It was more like pushing one open from the inside and finally being able to bask in treasure that had been there all along. I highly recommend it!

I reconnected with Kevin for lunch, and later that night we drove back to the church for the worship event. As Kevin made his way backstage, I chose an aisle seat at the back of the room so that it would be easier to move around and take pictures. By showtime, the tall, old theater was dimly lit and buzzing with ambient chatter, and children, and the sounds of instruments tuning up. As I scanned the seats around me, I couldn't help but smile when I noticed one attendee was warming up his trumpet so he could play along with the band.

About that time, I noticed a woman walking up the center aisle. She was smiling directly at me, so I readied myself to exchange hellos. She introduced herself as the mother-in-law of the gal who owned Jo's coffee shop and, because she also followed along with me online, revealed that she could completely relate to my struggle with anxiety and panic. Then she handed me a pocket-sized paperback book. It was called *Hope and Help for Your Nerves*. When she heard from her daughter-in-law that I was going to be at The Mission Church, she felt compelled to hand-deliver her copy. She said she had gleaned a great deal of wisdom and experienced an incredible amount of comfort in reading it. I remember feeling a little embarrassed, but I was also so touched by her thoughtful gesture. A few moments later, we hugged and then she made her way back to her seat. I scanned the front and back covers of the book before stuffing it into my purse. I didn't dare crack it open while we were so far away from home because I thought *reading* about anxiety would surely stir up a whole mess of it too.

When we got back to Alabama, it sat on my nightstand for weeks. I didn't want to jinx what felt like progress. I seemed to be doing so much better after having reset on the road.

But then one day, I found the courage to start reading it, and I realized by the end of the second page that I had been given an incredible gift. In her first sentence, the author, an Australian woman named Dr. Claire Weekes who lived from 1903 to 1990, promised to talk to me as if I were sitting right beside her. But honestly, as I moved from chapter to chapter, *so* many of the descriptions hit *so* close to home, I often forgot that it was her voice and not my own. I had a real lightbulb moment when I read, "Your illness is very much an illness of how you think. It is very much an illness of your attitude to fear, panic. You may think it is an illness of how you feel (it most certainly seems like this), but how you feel depends on how you think, on what you think. Because it is an illness of what you think, you can recover. *Thoughts that are keeping you ill can be changed*."[2]

Up until that point, no doctor, psychiatrist, therapist, author, or any other human being had boiled it down so clearly or summed it up so profoundly.

On the next page, Dr. Weekes says, "I have no illusions about you: I am not writing this book for the rare brave people, but for you, a sick, suffering, ordinary human with no more courage than the rest of us but—and this is the important thing—with the same unplumbed, unsuspected power in reserve as the rest of us."[3]

> *Unplumbed*: "not fully examined or explored," "not understood in depth"[4]
> *Unsuspected*: "not imagined possible."[5]

What a reassuring way to not only help readers identify exactly what they're struggling with but also to make sure they know they're no less whole than someone who *isn't* struggling with anxiety and panic. That was huge for me because, thanks to my unhealthy relationship with fear, I had gotten used to feeling inferior to almost everyone around me. The smiley, thicker-skinned people hopping on planes by themselves and driving around in cars alone. The capable people volunteering, and visiting their friends, and eating lunch with their kids at school. The Insta-people sharing from concerts, and conferences, and church. Add in the kind of upbringing that championed perfectionism, discouraged "unnecessary" emotions, and pooh-poohed downtime for physical illness and/or pain, and I think I had probably felt broken in comparison for a very long time.

> I've always tried to make a home for myself, but I have not felt at home in myself. I've worked hard at being the hero of my own life. But every time I checked the register of displaced persons, I was still on it.
>
> —JEANETTE WINTERSON

I soaked the whole book up in one sitting and discovered that almost all of it applied directly to my situation. At one point, I actually considered highlighting the paragraphs I *didn't* necessarily need to remember instead of the ones I did. Otherwise, it ran the risk of becoming a very yellow book. By the time I had completely finished it, the compassionate and once-anxious author had posthumously equipped me with a crystal-clear description of my condition and proved with her own life that it was entirely curable. And *boy*, did that information make a difference. Because when I'm having a panic attack, I tend not to believe it. I think I'll be stuck that way forever as my mind tries to protect me by pulling me away from myself.

> I should probably mention that panic at this point looked a lot different than it ended up looking in Dr. McLaughlin's office, which is why I was so confused and had to "start over" in a sense. Not really, because it was all the same animal, but it definitely played out in a more life-altering way, and I didn't initially believe I wasn't permanently broken by panic. It was Drew Linsalata and his book *The Anxious Truth* that helped me figure out what was going on after the Dr. McLaughlin episode. He has been instrumental in helping me get back on track and has even coached me through some crippling panic attacks in real-time.

Weekes's words weren't just sitting next to each other on the page, they were rubbing together as I read them, creating a compassionate vibration. She had been to the same hell I had, and her wisdom was forged by a fire that proved I wasn't stuck.

Again, it didn't instantly take all my fear of fear away, but for the first time in my life, I heard the resonance of my hurting heart unabashedly and wholly reflected. She grounded me with wisdom that carried weight. She helped me understand that I wasn't afraid of driving, or exploring, or buildings full of people. I was simply gluing fear of physical sensations to lots of other things. Almost everything, in fact. From appointments and airplanes to crowds of people and conversations with strangers. I even glued it to spending time by myself.

> Sometimes, coming home is driving shotgun with a rider who already knows the way.

But the truth is, those kinds of things weren't ever the source of my panic. I had simply created a new story about them, one that said, "That place or that experience made me panic, and since I don't like to panic, now I need to avoid it." Dr. Weekes (and later Drew Linsalata) helped me realize that I can be the same person on the open road to Texas that I am inside my house. My experience all boils down to the stories I tell myself. Because, make no mistake, the stories you tell yourself can create a powerful belief, and belief can create physical sensations. And although the physical sensations are real, they are made real by a story that is not.

When we understand a little about how our minds work and we have some guideposts on how to deal with our emotions in a healthy way, we not only build resilience, but we can thrive and, over time, find a sense of growth.

—DR. JULIE SMITH

So how do we rewrite the story? **One small step at a time.** In order for your brain to believe something different, it needs evidence. How do we create evidence? **Small, consistent doses of courage.** You don't have to slay the dragon in one swing, but you do have to pick up your sword. You do have to show up to the fight. And the more you pick up your sword and the more you show up to fight, the more evidence you create. Then after a while, your brain starts to believe the new evidence, that you are, in fact, okay.

I LOVE THIS SERVED WARM AND FOR BREAKFAST!

Aunt Chriss's Pumpkin Mocha Coffee Cake

NOTE FROM LAYLA: *Speaking of coffee and one of my favorite out-of-towners—you must try my Aunt Chriss's breakfast cake. What a delectable way to wake up!*

Photo by Aubrey Sieberg

NOTE FROM AUNT CHRISS: *Baking allows me to slow down. Measuring, sifting, and combining ingredients to create a delicious, warm, sweet treat is like therapy. Sharing the result is my favorite way to show love!*

Streusel

Ingredients:

½ c. packed brown sugar

⅓ c. rolled oats

¼ c. all-purpose flour

½ tsp. pumpkin pie spice

¼ c. butter, cold

Instructions:

In a medium bowl, combine brown sugar, rolled oats, flour, and pumpkin pie spice. Cut in butter until crumbly.

Drizzle

Ingredients:

1¼ c. powdered sugar

1 tsp. light-colored corn syrup

2–3 tbsp. cooled, strong-brewed coffee

Instructions:

In a small bowl, stir together powdered sugar and corn syrup. Stir in enough cooled, strong-brewed coffee to make drizzling consistency.

Cake

Ingredients:

5 eggs

2 tsp. instant coffee granules

1 8-oz. package cream cheese, softened

⅔ c. sugar

2 tbsp. all-purpose flour

1 tsp. vanilla

3 c. all-purpose flour

2 tsp. baking powder

1 tsp. pumpkin pie spice

½ tsp. baking soda

½ tsp. salt

½ c. butter, softened

1½ c. sugar

⅔ c. canned 100% pure pumpkin (not pumpkin pie filling)

1 c. buttermilk

½ c. chopped walnuts

1 c. Ghirardelli 60% Cacao Bittersweet Premium Baking Chips

Instructions:

1. Preheat oven to 350 degrees. Grease a 13x9x2-inch baking pan; set aside.

2. In a small bowl, stir together 2 of the eggs and the instant coffee; set aside.

3. In a medium bowl, beat cream cheese with an electric mixer on medium speed until fluffy. Beat in ⅔ cup sugar, 2 tablespoons flour, and vanilla until smooth. Beat in egg/instant coffee mixture; set aside.

4. In a medium bowl, stir together remaining flour, baking powder, pumpkin pie spice, baking soda, and salt; set aside.

5. In a large bowl, beat butter with an electric mixer on medium speed for 30 seconds; gradually add remaining sugar, beating until fluffy. Add remaining eggs, 1 at a time, beating well after each. Beat in pumpkin. Alternately add flour mixture and buttermilk to pumpkin mixture, beating after each addition until combined. Fold in nuts and baking chips.

6. Spread half of the batter in the prepared baking pan. Drop half of the cream cheese mixture in small spoonfuls on top of batter. Add remaining batter in spoonfuls; carefully spread over cream cheese mixture. Top with spoonfuls of

the remaining cream cheese mixture. With a knife, swirl batter to marble. Sprinkle with streusel.

7. Bake in preheated oven for 45 to 50 minutes or until a toothpick inserted near center comes out clean. Cool in pan on a wire rack for 45 minutes. Spoon drizzle over cake. Cool completely on wire rack.

WHAT A SURPRISE TO FIND A SMILE INSIDE!

FROM KEVIN

How to Change Someone's Life

In 2013, researchers conducted an experiment in high school English classrooms. The students were told to write an essay about their personal hero. The teachers were instructed to give half of the class normal feedback, and the other half of the class an extra sentence of additional feedback. The study showed that one year later, the students who received the extra feedback were doing significantly better in English.

What was the one extra sentence?

"I am giving you this feedback because I believe in you."⁶

Why did that one sentence have such a significant impact a whole year later? Because it changed what the students believed about themselves, and belief is more powerful than most of us realize.

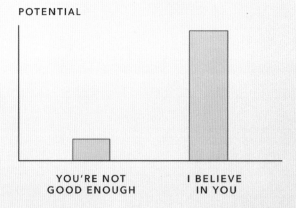

WORDS MATTER

POTENTIAL

YOU'RE NOT GOOD ENOUGH   I BELIEVE IN YOU

Words Matter: The Power of Belief

I was reminded of this study recently during a conversation with Layla when (noticing that I was struggling with something) she said, "I believe in you." Four simple words, but the positive impact they had on me can't be measured. She could see something in me that I was having trouble seeing in myself, and because I trust her opinion, her words created a new belief in me.

When the flame inside of us is starting to go out, a word of encouragement is like oxygen.

Trust is a key factor in this. I trust Layla's opinion because, after nearly twenty years of marriage, she knows me so well.

Words from someone we trust can help us create belief.

Belief can become the fuel that guides our decisions and propels us into action.

Actions can create our future.

It all starts with an idea and the belief that it's possible.

> Whether you think you can do a thing or not, you are right.
> —attributed to Henry Ford

The Dark Side of Belief

Like most things that hold power, our beliefs have the ability to propel us forward or hold us back. I often wonder how many dreams have been cut short because someone was told that they didn't have enough talent, or they'd never be good enough.

In Benjamin Hardy's book _Personality Isn't Permanent_, he shares about a conversation he had with a woman named Rosalie. Fifty years prior, Rosalie dreamed of writing and illustrating a children's book and decided to take a big first step by signing up for art classes at a local studio. One night during an art class with a handful of other people, Rosalie had an experience that ended her dream. After a particular drawing exercise, the teacher went around the room checking each student's work. When he stopped at Rosalie, he grabbed her chalk and "corrected" her drawing.

During the sixty or so seconds that the teacher was drawing over her work, Rosalie felt extremely embarrassed. None of the other students had been corrected in this manner. All eyes were on her. This was all too painful for her to handle. In the emotional swirl of the moment, a thought entered her mind: _I must not be very good at this._

Rosalie never attempted drawing again.[7]

Although the art teacher never actually said anything to Rosalie, she trusted his opinion, and his actions (likely unintentionally) created a belief in her that she wasn't good at drawing.

That may seem extreme to some folks reading this, but I'd be willing to bet that all of us are lugging around some "little" belief that keeps our foot firmly planted on an invisible brake pedal too.

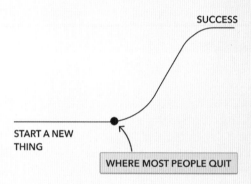

KEEP GOING

SUCCESS

START A NEW THING

WHERE MOST PEOPLE QUIT

The Truth about What's Possible

Here's the good news: Most of us are capable of doing much more than we think. In the beginning stages of learning something new, it can seem frustrating and nearly impossible to do that new thing. But time and time again, research has shown that hard work and consistency have much more to do with a person's skill level and success than simply being born with talent. That doesn't mean that there aren't people who have more natural ability in certain areas; it just means that with determination, consistency, and time, we can achieve much more than we probably realize. And sometimes we just need to hear, "You're doing great." Those kinds of words can plant seeds of belief. And it's what you choose to believe that makes you the person you are. So keep moving confidently in the direction of your dreams, reader. I believe in you!

coming home is . . .
a choice

Only when we are brave enough to explore the darkness will we discover the infinite power of our light.

—Brené Brown

A couple of years ago, Kevin and I decided to go out on a date. It was during the height of my struggle with agoraphobia, which made it incredibly hard not to panic in busy places, but it had been years since the two of us had eaten dinner alone, and I *really* wanted a Crazy Roll from Osaka. If you've never had one, it's a delectable deep-fried, foot-long log of white rice, wrapped in nori, and sliced to reveal layers of colorful seafood, cream cheese, and avocado. I know. Heaven on a platter, right? It's served with yum yum sauce that, honestly, couldn't have a more appropriate name. Kevin, on the other hand, won't touch sushi with a ten-foot pole but, thankfully, he's wild about chicken teriyaki and lives for the ambiance of a dimly lit restaurant.

So, armed with my cravings and just enough confidence to try, I marched next door to our in-laws' place and asked Kevin's mom if she would watch Steevenson while we went out to eat. Once she gave us the green light, Kevin and I dashed upstairs to brush our hair and climb into more presentable clothes. I chose a black cotton sundress dotted with tiny white flowers and a denim button-up shirt, tied at my waist. I slid into my favorite pair of black leather sandals and tried my best to ignore the anticipatory anxiety that had begun screaming at me to stay home.

As I brushed my teeth, my thoughts swung wildly between how fun the night should be and how awful it could be. That's one of the worst parts of being controlled by an anxiety disorder: the shame that comes along with the "should be." It's just as damaging as the fear that comes along with the "could be." The "should be" reveals that, in addition to feeling afraid, you're also struggling with a major lack of self-worth. Because you "shouldn't" feel this way. It's not normal. It's not acceptable. It's not what your spouse signed up for. It's not what your kids need from you. It's not what your friends want from you. It's not who you want to be.

I finally told Kevin I was worrying on the way out to the car, and because he is understanding, he quickly tried to assure me that everything would be okay either way. My mind continued to race all the way to town, but I tried my best to enjoy the beautiful view. The birds lined up like notes on a staff, and the clouds unspooling in the clean blue air. The neat rows of crops between the tree lines on either side of us, with puffy bolls of cotton popping forth across the top.

Once we got to the restaurant, a quaint little hole-in-the-wall sandwiched in the middle of a long strip of shops, I had all but convinced myself I would start to hyperventilate once I went inside. I hemmed and hawed for several minutes once Kevin shut off the engine and I got way too caught up in the "what if" narrative doing laps in my head. I kicked myself for not taking a Xanax while I was getting ready at home. I kicked myself again for my irrational fear of medications. Kevin may have asked me if we should just go to a drive-through and eat in the car, but all I heard was, "I LOVE THIS RESTAURANT, AND I AM SO EXCITED TO EAT CHICKEN TERIYAKI HERE TONIGHT! IT IS GOING TO BE SO FUN TO SIT IN A BOOTH WITH MY SUPER BRAVE WIFE!"

So into Osaka we went, and I was more in my head than ever as our unsuspecting hostess showed us to our table—the most private booth in the place. Thankfully, it was nestled right up against a front window, so after a quick twist of the mini blind rod before our server arrived, I was able to see our car on the other side of the glass, just a few steps away. For people who struggle with agoraphobia (a disorder that involves a specific anxiety about being in a place or situation where escape is difficult or embarrassing), being able to get out quickly is paramount. We develop an unhealthy and unhelpful relationship with control in order to avoid all the scary-to-us physical sensations that come along with panicking.

A waitress skittered up to our table a moment later, completely unaware that she was interrupting a conversation about whether or not we were even going to stay. I quickly rattled off something about not feeling well and asked her if she could give us a minute before we ordered our drinks. She nearly tripped over my left foot as she scurried away, confused. That's when I noticed my entire left leg and butt cheek still hadn't committed to our booth. Once the coast was clear, I stood up so that I could be closer to the floor-to-ceiling window. I took a deep breath and begged my brain to understand that the only thing separating me from the "safety" of our car was a quarter-inch sheet of glass.

I pleaded with my adrenaline to stop coursing, but naturally that just made it course faster. As I turned to sit back down, I noticed the floor felt spongy beneath my feet, and all of a sudden, my depth perception went wonky too. The amalgamation of voices, and music, and silverware, and sizzling food intensified to near deafening. I lowered myself back down onto the booth seat so that I wouldn't fall over (because surely fainting was the next step, right?), and the second my eyes met Kevin's, I started to cry. Without a sound, my mouth and my shoulders melted toward the floor, and the tears I had been holding in since before we left the house finally came. A few seconds later, our waitress tentatively poked her head around the tall seat back behind me. I looked up and saw that she was doing that thing with her face that people do when they don't know if they should even ask. That thing where you stretch the left and right sides of your mouth down and out to expose your bottom row of gritted teeth. I quickly fanned my face to really drive home the fact that I "wasn't feeling well." Then, impulsively and unbeknownst to Kevin, I told her we had decided to leave. Hearing this, she flew into action, nodding and smiling nervously as she began to scoop up our menus so that she could be anywhere but there. I stood up and started walking away before she had even finished. That's when I noticed the room had been emptied of all its gravity, and I struggled with disequilibrium all the way back to the front door.

We drove a Nissan Rogue at the time, and I was already standing with my hand on the passenger door handle by the time Kevin came out. I felt taut. Swollen with fear. Full of what felt like an invisible, combustible energy—like a tire hooked up to an air pump way too long. *Why did sitting in one of my favorite restaurants have to be so unbearable? Will I EVER be able to do things without panicking again?!* The questions were as sharp as fishhooks, and the answers felt impossible. It had been almost a decade since I had read Dr. Weekes's book (and I hadn't yet met Drew), so I guess this heightened level of panic made me believe this situation was different. Kevin used the key fob to open our doors, and I shattered into a thousand pieces the second I sat down. Tears exploded from my eyes, and I screamed at myself for ruining everything as Kevin calmly drove us away. He took us in the opposite direction of our house, but I didn't even notice. I was busy barreling somewhere else. Somewhere sunless and barren. A place I had never been to before. As our car snaked around the edge of the city, I sat slumped and sobbing in the passenger seat. Wailing all my worries into my hands so that Kevin couldn't see my humiliated face. He never said a word. He knew I just needed time to detonate. And when I finally ran out of breath, I stared off into middle distance, vacant and shriveled, until eventually I was completely hollowed of hope.

Several moments later, the sound of Kevin's voice flickered in the darkness like a small, warm flame. I had almost forgotten he was there.

"Do you want to go home?" he asked from some faraway place on my left.

"I don't think I can," I replied almost inaudibly.

It was not the answer Kevin was expecting, and honestly, it wasn't how I was expecting to feel in that moment either. "I feel like if I go home right now, I'm not ever going to leave again. I'm just going to tell you and everyone else that I'm done. That agoraphobia won." Saying it out loud seemed to divide time because, all of a sudden, I realized that I was at a crossroads, not actually barreling toward some pathless world of despair. I was at an intersection. In one direction, I imagined a dark and snarling future that threatened to swallow me whole. In the other, an opportunity to rewrite the narrative and an unexpected boost of willpower. It was as if emptying myself of all those negative thoughts and emotions had created room for the calm and courage that was there all along. I could clearly see that I had a choice to make.

> After discharging painful emotions, verbally or nonverbally, we can usually think more clearly. Heavy emotions tend to bend the mind out of shape. This emotional clearance is like clearing the air or silencing a deafening noise. An overload of emotions almost always obscures one's vision beyond recognition.
>
> —JOHN JOSEPH POWELL

The discovery instantly began to replenish me with hope, and I surprised us both when, just a few moments later, I told Kevin I was ready to try a different restaurant. He made a U-turn at the next light and took us to Tazikis. We linked arms and strode across the parking lot together, and when we reached the door, I felt strangely eager to go inside. My face was puffy from crying, but I smiled all the way up to the service counter. I kept my swollen eyes hidden from the gal at the register by studying their menu like I had never seen it before, and once we had placed our order, we sat down at a table near the door.

For the better part of an hour, we talked, and ate, and celebrated my unforeseen victory. I wasn't completely free of anxiety, but I was no longer bracing against it. I surrendered to the ambient noise around us and relaxed my face and body whenever I noticed a part of me was tense. The floor didn't bounce when I got up to refill my drink, and I never felt the urge to race back outside. It was just me and my favorite person, on a dinner date at a different-than-planned, dimly lit restaurant. It felt miraculous. It was as if all of my feelings about fear had spilled out and, in turn, I was less afraid.

I'm still continually learning to surrender to the physical sensations that can come along with panic, but it's true what they say about bottling things up: **Sometimes, breaking down is really the bravest thing you can do.** It takes guts to let go and lay yourself out so completely that your only (and potentially awesome) option is to finally decide how you want to put yourself back together. And, by the way, crying hard doesn't mean you're crazy. It just means that you're on your own side.

Which reminds me, in case no one has told you lately, struggling with fear doesn't mean you're weak. It means you're human. A living, learning, resilient human who is wired for growth and change. Don't let anyone tell you otherwise—especially not your thoughts. Because remember, it's in the doing, not the thinking, that transformation can truly take place.

How To Get from Here to There

Go Slow

Studies show that exposure therapy is one of the most effective ways to treat fear and retrain your brain, so start by giving yourself permission to ease back into it. There is a more intense method called flooding, where you literally subject yourself to the things that scare you full-force until they don't anymore, but I will always prefer the more effective/less stressful method, because it's, well, more effective and less stressful. In the case of the sushi restaurant, Osaka, I started by simply riding past "the scene of the crime." I would imagine myself going inside and set that goal in my mind's eye. After some time had passed, and I had moved further away from the trauma, Kevin and I started eating lunch (from somewhere else—ha!) in the car in the parking lot outside Osaka. Not every day, although that probably would have significantly sped up my recovery process. Then, one day, when the weather was gorgeous and my craving for sushi had grown stronger than my desire to avoid it, we sat at one of their outdoor tables and enjoyed a sushi (and chicken teriyaki!) dinner. We did that a couple more times before I decided to try feeling uncomfortable inside, and eventually, and with consistency, I was able to show my brain that it *was* possible to enjoy Osaka. I leaned into discomfort just enough to make it slowly fade away.

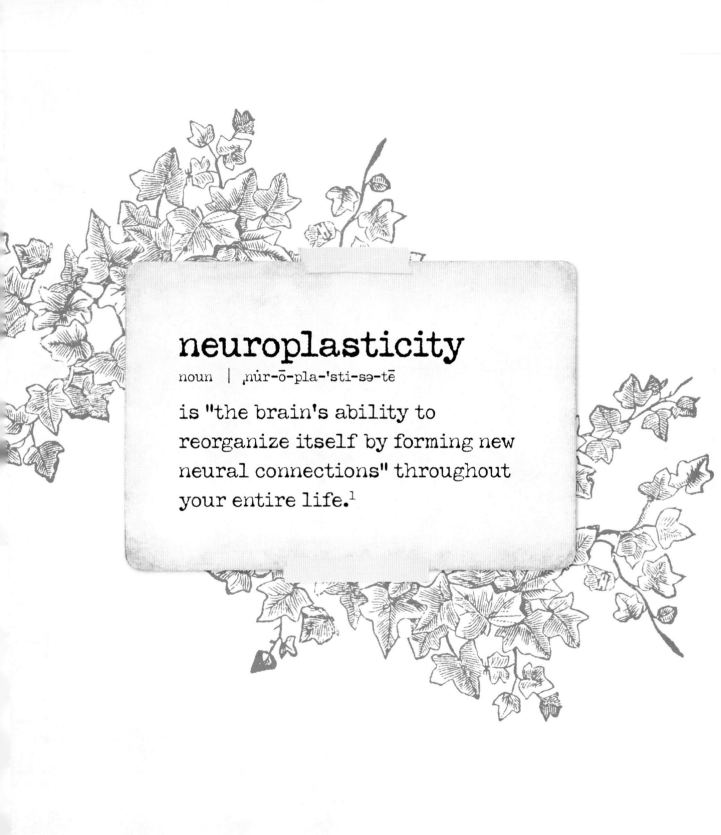

neuroplasticity

noun | ˌnu̇r-ō-pla-ˈsti-sə-tē

is "the brain's ability to reorganize itself by forming new neural connections" throughout your entire life.[1]

> Eventually the most remarkable thing happened: I began to change, learning how to accept life just enough that I didn't have to dart for the nearest escape hatch every time things got uncomfortable.
>
> —JILLIAN LAUREN

It's never too late to learn (or unlearn!) a certain way of thinking or behaving, and thanks to the ongoing process of neuroplasticity, our brains always have the ability to adapt and change.

> If you've reinforced a thought pattern or habit for years or decades, it can seem like it's just "who you are." But it's just a well-reinforced network in your brain—it can be overwritten.
>
> —KEVIN ESPIRITU

Hang Loose

Like I mentioned at the beginning of this book, hearing "just calm down" isn't usually helpful when it comes to actually calming down, but I have found that if you choose to put that suggestion into practice *regularly*—and before you actually need to calm down—it can soften your experience with the kind of anxiety that can lead to panic. In other words, when I got in the habit of setting aside time to relax my body and focus on breathing daily when I *wasn't* anxious, it became second nature to do those things whenever I *was* anxious, which would often lead to a de-escalation of my racing thoughts and scary-to-me physical sensations. Learning to auto-relax my body and belly breathe has helped me calm down countless times. While stuck in traffic, standing in a long line, or upon waking suddenly at 2 a.m.—when, for some reason, everything suddenly seems so urgent and insurmountable. Using these built-in abilities in response to mounting anxiety is a very effective way to quiet those sudden and intrusive thoughts that do their best to keep propelling you toward overwhelmed and afraid.

Do the Opposite

Being told to "just think positive" can also feel like a super-unhelpful suggestion in the midst of a stressful season, because recovery from an anxiety disorder (or any kind of anxiety, really) doesn't happen by simply replacing our negative thoughts with positive ones. Recovery requires thinking differently *about* our negative thoughts. **It's about rooting our response to anxiety in curiosity, not control.** Because, ironically, the more we let go of control, the more control we will have. By responding to our negative thoughts, sensations, and circumstances from a more flexible, inquisitive place, we give our brains the chance to form new, evidence-based beliefs. That way, it's not just about thinking an unreliable thought, it's about potentially experiencing actual change. One effective way to do that is to do the opposite. When my friend (and panic disorder overcomer) Drew Linsalata first suggested this method, I thought it sounded a little bit like flooding, but it's not nearly that intense. As he describes in *The Anxious Truth* (a must-read if you struggle with panic), it's as simple as this: If your tendency to avoid something is because of an irrational fear, be intentional about taking baby steps toward it, versus away from it.[2] So, for instance, if that pesky, anxious voice in your head says, "Stay busy because sitting still will just give you more time to (negatively) think."

Choose to do the opposite. Sit down and loosen your (likely tense) body. Yes, you are anxious, but your brain needs you to physically show it you're not in danger. I promise, if the question is "How will I ever move past this fear of fear?" The answer is smack-dab in the middle of that question. By intentionally moving *past* it. Anything else is avoidance, and that's not going to help you overcome things. Think of it like the world's widest trip wire. You can either spend your whole life trying to figure out what it's tied to, only to find that loosening that knot won't make the wire go away, or you can see it for what it is and begin baby-stepping to the other side of it. You may be surprised at how quickly you can turn around and look back.

> **Repeat after Joshua Fletcher (@AnxietyJosh) next time you start to panic:**
>
> "Okay. This is just adrenaline. This is cortisol. It's going to increase my heart rate, my breathing is going to change slightly and everything is going to feel detached and weird. I might feel tension, tingling. My thoughts are probably racing. It's okay. It's just adrenaline and cortisol. Maybe I'm lightheaded. Maybe I've got ectopic beats. Maybe I feel a bit nauseous. It's okay. It's just adrenaline and cortisol. This will pass, it always passes. The body can only produce a finite amount of adrenaline and cortisol, and I'll feel all right at the end of it. I can get through this. I don't need to run and escape. *I am* the coping technique, and this will pass."

FROM KEVIN

I was with Layla the whole time she was panicking in the restaurant but I didn't fully understand what she was going through at the time because she put so much energy into keeping it together. Reading her story about it later helped me realize that there is always more than one battle going on. Not only does she deal with physical sensations that feel like they are going to kill her, but she also puts an extreme amount of energy into what's happening on the outside and, honestly, she has developed such an art form of holding it together that, even to this day, I can't always identify when she's struggling. My perception of her at Osaka, until she erupted in the car, was that of an uneasy, polite, and apologetic girl. I didn't realize she was also worried about what everyone around her might think if her sensations intensified too much to keep hidden. **It's two battles.** She's trying to save herself, <u>and</u> she's trying to not let anyone know that she's trying to save herself.

coming home is . . .
treading lightly
through tender places

Sometimes, reaching out and taking someone's hand is the beginning of a journey. At other times, it is allowing another to take yours.

—Vera Nazarian

Sometimes, it's both at the exact same time.

—Layla Palmer

It had to be a hundred degrees outside the day we met our daughter, Meme, at an outdoor event called Camp Hope. I was sweating bullets for another reason, though, and I had a real I-don't-know-if-I-can-do-this moment between our car and the camp lodge. We were still fifty feet from the action, but my ears were already ringing, and because I was struggling with agoraphobia, I honestly didn't know if I could walk into such a busy building without losing my balance and forgetting how to breathe.

But that particular day in May 2019, I was **so** determined to at least try. I hadn't been anywhere that mattered in months, and I knew that hiding forever would only make it harder to find myself or show up for anybody else.

> I want to be the best version of myself for anyone who is going to someday walk into my life and need someone to love them beyond reason.
>
> —JENNIFER ELISABETH

The lodge was packed with volunteers and kids of all ages who had found themselves in the foster care system, including Meme. We were immediately directed toward a row of folding tables covered in stacks of bright red volunteer T-shirts and rows of handwritten name badges. As we stood in line, we listened to the lead organizer explain how the day would go, and when her instructions came to an end, we were invited to change our shirts in one of the windowless restrooms in the hallway. I felt even more trapped once I was half-naked (*you can't escape if you're not fully dressed!*), and I was still front-tucking my volunteer tee and pulling my lanyard over my head as I quickly burst back out through the door.

Once everyone else had casually trickled out and gathered on the gigantic lawn, organizers began to call out names and instructions, so that everybody knew where to go and what to do. Kevin and I were told that we were going to be in charge of the two-year-olds group, and Steevenson was invited to fish with the seven-year-olds, who were already on their way down to the lake. Meme was also assigned to our team, and I remember feeling like I was in the presence of an actual angel when she floated over to us.

"She's from Haiti," our mutual friend Sonia said, as she introduced us to the sunniest girl I had ever seen. She was shy, and very quiet, but I could tell that her wide, closemouthed smile was dying to reveal its pretty, pearly-white teeth. Her eyes sparkled when we told her our son was also Haitian, and we tried to impress her with our clunky Creole as we walked together across the lawn. In a matter of moments, and without exchanging more than a handful of words, it felt like I had known her my whole life.

> She speaks with her eyes. She moves like the breeze. When she laughs the world stops for a while.
>
> —AVIJEET DAS

We had six busy toddlers to wrangle between the three of us. Half of them were runners, and bless their hearts, the other half insisted on being held.

The camp was sectioned into several outdoor play stations, and our groups were supposed to rotate every half hour or so. Station 1 was a couple of kiddie pools filled with sand and colorful toys to build and dig with. It looked like a good time to me, but not everyone loved it, so Kevin and Meme took turns retrieving the runners that kept escaping to Station 2. It had three inflatable slides, one netted bouncy house, and at least four extra kids that had gotten away from their groups too.

Station 3 was the only one covered by large vendor tents. There were two kiddie pools filled with water underneath one, and a couple of folding tables smothered in squirt guns under the other. When it wasn't our turn to be there, I *pined* for Station 3. It had shade, and less-hot grass, and offered the occasional splash of lukewarm water. It was the sacred and alluring waterpark that sprung from the center of Camp Hope, and I found myself counting the minutes in between shifts. It didn't end up being the kids' favorite, though, because they weren't allowed to actually get **into** the water. None of them were wearing swimsuits, and all of them were wearing regular diapers. I was sad for the kids that someone had forgotten to send that memo.

Which brings me to Station 4: the restroom. Okay, the bathroom in the lunchroom wasn't technically a station, but it was big and air-conditioned. And although I don't have a whole lot of experience wiping other people's butts, it was a chance to get out of the heat and to set a child (or two) down for a bit. It was a much-appreciated retreat, and all throughout the day, cooled-off group leaders would reemerge into the hundred-degree heat covered in goosebumps and not even caring that they might smell a little like poop.

After lunch, we were joined by a late arrival; a taller and talkative little boy who repeatedly made sure we all knew he was three. For the next few hours, he and our active two-year-olds darted from station to station while the rest of us scrambled behind them like tin cans tied to a getaway car. Eventually, we gave up trying to stick together as one unit, and Kevin, Meme, and I just careened around after the kids as they ran off in different directions. We waved and exchanged exhausted expressions with each other from afar and, if I'm honest, we checked our phones for the time whenever we could sneak a peek.

Near the end of the day, our group reconvened at the picnic table area so the kids would all be together when their foster parents arrived to pick them up. Meme and I spotted some rocking chairs on a covered porch near the lunchroom, so we poured ourselves into them and topped our legs with the little ones who were still happiest on our laps.

> Beginning to live as though there's no such thing as other people's children might be our most critical, significant contribution to the flourishing of our own world.
>
> —SHANNAN MARTIN

As we rocked, I asked Meme questions that I had been dying to deep dive on all day. I wanted to hear about her school and her hobbies, and I really just wanted *her* to have a chance to talk. I wanted *her* to feel like she was cared for at Camp Hope too. She told me about her favorite foods, and her biological family, and about the time she got to march in the Rose Bowl parade with her school band. She told me she'd be eighteen in one week, and because she seemed eager to absorb them, I told her stories about our visits to Haiti. She hadn't been back since her family moved to Florida when she was six. Her smile came alive when I described the Angel House and meeting Steevenson for the first time. Then, when we were too tired to even talk, we just swayed in the wet heat, side by side, and, as far as I was concerned, inexplicably certain we were destined to meet. At one point, and out of habit, I scanned myself for anxiety, but I couldn't find any. It was just me and my excitement to learn more about this reserved yet responsive girl. It felt foreign and remarkable, just like her.

Around 5 o'clock, grateful grown-ups began scooping up their sticky, sun-kissed kids, and Steevenson came back up the hill shouting, "AND GUESS WHAT?! WE DIDN'T CATCH ANY FISH!!" We all had a good chuckle, and it served as a funny icebreaker as we introduced him to Meme. They're ten years apart, so they didn't click like kids who are closer in age might have, but I think I knew right then that they would eventually become some kind of siblings. I couldn't see the whole staircase, of course, but all of a sudden, it was as if I were looking back down through a doorway from atop a big and very important first step. The feeling didn't make much sense logistically at the time because she lived in a group home four hours north of us, but I felt it nonetheless.

And then there was my pesky panic disorder. I mean, sure, I had made it through *that* day without having an attack and hightailing it back home, but I remember thinking, *How on earth could I handle **all** the things that come along with building a new relationship* and *potentially becoming someone's mentor or adoptive mom?*

We all have those moments though, right? The ones where we feel equal parts impassioned and unequipped. Half on fire for something (or someone) and half freaked out and frozen stiff. John Lennon once said, "There are two basic motivating forces: fear and love. When we are afraid, we pull back from life. When we are in love, we open to all that life has to offer with passion, excitement, and acceptance. . . . All hopes for a better world rest in the fearlessness and open-hearted vision of people who embrace life."[1] . . . I love that. Except I'd replace the word *fearlessness* with *bravefullness*. I know, I know. It's not a real word, but if we have to be completely void of fear to live life to the fullest, we may not ever try to do it.

I think it's okay to feel afraid. Just like it's okay to feel mad, happy, or sad. I mean, who decided we should be ashamed of feeling scared? And why do we beat ourselves up so much for being anxious?

> To aim for brave-FULL (or at least partially full—ha!) versus always striving to be fear-LESS, we cultivate an honest kind of courage, and that kind of vulnerability can become the wings that carry us to freedom.

And luckily, there's no right or wrong way to be brave. It's really just deciding that something important to you is more important than fear. So how I let go of fear will likely look different from how you let go of it, but taking a step outside of our comfort zones shouldn't ever be something we feel bad about. Because when it comes to our moxie, we get to be like Picasso—who decided that the eyes don't have to be where the eyes really are, and a nose can sit somewhere else too. Picasso's cubist art is his adventurous interpretation of a face, and by allowing ourselves that same kind of leeway, our vulnerability and experiences can be painted by the color of *our* courage too.

Don't worry if people think you're crazy. You are crazy. You have that kind of intoxicating insanity that lets other people dream outside of the lines and become who they're destined to be.

—JENNIFER ELISABETH

Meme asked me to be her mentor exactly two months from that first day we met. I'll never forget it. It was the Fourth of July, and we were standing under a sky full of fireworks when she popped the question—the one to which neither of us really knew what the answer yes meant.

Looking back, I think it was just a fancy, less awkward way for a 17-year-old to ask, "Wanna be friends?" And now that we're four years in, I realize that saying yes to a mentorship with Meme gave me an opportunity to become a compassionate witness—someone who shows up and stays present with someone who needs love and support—and in doing so, I opened myself up to those same kindnesses in return. Sure, we've had some growing pains along the way, but who doesn't? Aren't we all supposed to be in the ongoing business of forgiving faults and uncovering feelings we didn't know existed? Together, Meme and I are learning to tread lightly through tender places and to trust that things will fall into place without either of us forcing them there.

We received Meme's adoption decree in the mail on October 7, 2021. After nearly a year of praying about how to proceed, researching adult adoption, meeting with attorneys, and chasing a variety of documents—another kind judge, in another unknown room, at another unknown time, signed his name on the piece of paper that officially made us family. Meme cried with a smile, and then without one, when we told her the news, and the invisible fault line created by two deeply contrasting emotions wasn't lost on me. Because, sometimes, coming home is tending to old wounds by trusting new beginnings.

coming home is . . .
soft fascination

I want to have a little house
with sunlight on the floor,
A chimney with a rosy hearth
and lilacs by the door.

—Nancy Byrd Turner[1]

It was a cold and mushy April Fool's Day in 1983 when my family made the move from a starter home in the city to a hobby farm in the country.

Sometimes, I close my eyes just so I can fly around that old place in my mind. The house, an American Foursquare built in 1920, was frosted in thick, white stucco and topped with the sweet added touch of dormer roofs. Our acreage was wedge-shaped, and the elevation rolled and sloped like the top of an overstuffed pie.

The property needed a lot of love when we first moved in, and some of the outbuildings and the gigantic third-floor attic were still full of the original owner's sixty-year-old stuff.

MY CHILDHOOD HOME

I love a place like that, don't you? So full of stories (its own *and* its occupants') that its personality is almost human? Its front becomes a face; its closets become its pockets. (We've got a quirky, twenty-foot-tall stone fireplace in our current home, and I haven't had the heart to change it yet because it feels like my living room's nose—ha!)

My mom got straight to work tidying up the oval-shaped flower bed near the front of the house—tulips in the center flanked by two giant lilac bushes on each end. I used to love burying my face in the thick fluff of its tiny blossoms; the scent was a milky medley of rose, vanilla, almond, and fresh green leaves—*mmmm!* Sometimes, I wonder if they're still there. When I was little, my friend Kwenen nicknamed me "Layla Lilac" because I loved them (and the color lavender) so much.

Another outdoor highlight was the just-for-fun flower garden out back. You could see it through the kitchen

ADVICE FROM
A LILAC:

Create a colorful life.

Drink plenty of water.

Enjoy the sunshine.

Be flexible.

Open up.

Make new buds.

Take time to smell
the flowers . . .
especially lilacs!

HOW 'BOUT THEM APPLES?
I SPY OUR LITTLE CLUBHOUSE
BEHIND THE WINDMILL TOO!

window above our hardworking sink. The garden was rectangular, and Mom created it so we could (almost) always have fresh arrangements and a room with a rainbow-colored view. Except for in winter, when the earth hardened and hid beneath blankets of snow until spring. There was just enough space for two rows of fruit trees beyond that garden, so Mom planted State Fair apples. It was a farm-to-face kind of deal as far as my brother and I were concerned, and when we were full, we'd feed our apple cores to the horses, whose pasture sat at one end of the flower garden, or to our dogs, whose outdoor kennel run sat at the other. (The Labradors, by the way, were both sweet as could be, but if left to their own devices while my parents were at work, they would dash over to the neighbor's pig farm and swim in the "lagoon." Ew!)

Beyond the apple trees stood the old windmill that had
been there since the farm's beginning, and a hodgepodge,
one-room clubhouse my handy grandpa cobbled together
for me and my brother. He had seen us attempting to build
one with some leftover wood one day and sprang into action
when he realized we were struggling. The finished product
had built-in bunks, two functional windows, and a pitched
roof clad in real shingles. It was perfect, and it proved to me
that even grown-ups can see magic if they just take the time
to look for it.

We plastered the walls with stickers, and drawings, and
pages torn from our favorite magazines, and at some point, I
connected our clubhouse to the garage with a series of exten-
sion cords so I could watch soap operas on a tiny TV.

There was a half-acre patch of strawberries in one corner
of our six-acre lot and, starting that very first spring, Mom
was determined to ready its rows by June. She was an architectural draftsperson by day but spent many an evening
pulling weeds. I can still see her out there, surrounded by
rows of happy green leaves, on her knees in her after-work
jeans.

A week or so before that first season, I painted "Come Pick Strawberries!" on big squares of leftover plywood. I embellished the corners with happy red berries, and as soon as the paint was dry, Dad secured my signs to tall, sturdy steel posts. He planted them wherever the surrounding highways met the gravel roads that stretched back to our house, and I used to feel so proud of myself when we'd pass by them on the way to and from town.

Initially, my parents had no idea what kind of crowds to expect, but they learned very quickly that Minnesotans love fresh strawberries, and they'll show up before dawn to pick 'em. All day long, pickers squeezed their cars past each other on the single-lane road that snaked to and from our patch. It was so fun to be around grown-ups who got bound-out-of-bed excited about a little red fruit!

Photos by Ruth Klossner

"MY" LITTLE SIGN IN OUR "BIG" NEWSPAPER

We were open for eight days every June, and we had two varieties for folks to fill their pails with: Stoplight and Trumpeter. They were vivid, and juicy, and great for freezing. Mom stuffed them inside pies, piled them onto shortcake, and squashed them into jam that made warm toast taste just like summer. My fondest memory is of eating them straight from the patch.

After the sixth season, my mom decided to switch gears and grow Christmas trees instead, but to this day, I still can't see a strawberry without thinking of her.

Things My Mom Would Tell Her 37-Year-Old Self

1. **Some of those crazy, heart-stopping fears you have are really just crazy.** Red lights on your car dash do not always mean IMMINENT DANGER: CAR ABOUT TO IMPLODE. Dentists are there to help, not hurt. Dogs and horses that run away almost always come back for food. Overflowing toilets only get worse if you run. Wasps are very small and can be smooshed if necessary, and seaweed is not an underwater monster trying to drown you—it's just seaweed. (PS: At fifty-seven, you will hardly fear anything at all!)

2. **You need to take care of your body.** Brush and floss—MOISTURIZE—stretch and exercise—MOISTURIZE—drink lots of water—MOISTURIZE—eat unprocessed foods—MOISTURIZE. Vanity aside, at fifty-seven, you will have a lot of things left to do on your bucket list that will require you to be in relatively good physical condition for several more years.

3. **Money for retirement requires planning and diligence.**
   Remind your children of this often. Also, quite a few of
   your bucket list items will cost some money. If you save ten
   dollars per week over the next twenty years, you'll have over
   ten thousand "bucket list bucks" when you're fifty-seven.

4. **Almost-adult children need help deciding how to make their
   way into the real (big) world when they leave the nest.**
   Spend lots of time helping them learn their strengths and
   passions so they can have a successful, enjoyable career,
   and take care of themselves in any lifestyle they dream of.
   When you feel totally unqualified or need answers, search
   out capable guidance professionals, mentors, ministers,
   hypnotists—somebody! The old saying about moms "being as
   happy as their unhappiest child" is very true.

5. **Family and close friend relationships need cultivating.** Dig:
   Find the real stuff. Aerate: Expel the issues. Renew: Forgive,
   it enlarges the future. Keep in touch, even if it means just
   being there to listen. Everyone needs, and deserves, people
   to catch them when they fall, and to cheer them on when
   they're finding their footing.

*Treasure your relationships,
not your possessions.*
—Anthony J. D'Angelo

Jude's Foldover Cookies

NOTE FROM JUDE: *These cookies were always a hit at Christmastime! I've never liked to eat a lot of sugar, so I always thought they were such a fun way to get the whole taste of a pie in one tiny bite.*

Ingredients:

1½ c. all-purpose flour
¼ c. granulated sugar
¼ tsp. ground allspice

¾ c. softened butter
⅓ c. sour cream
1 beaten egg yolk

Instructions:

1. Combine flour, sugar, and allspice; cut in butter until mixture resembles fine crumbs.

2. In a separate bowl, combine sour cream and egg yolk, then blend them into the flour mixture.

3. Divide dough into 2 portions and form them into balls. Cover each with plastic wrap and chill several hours or overnight. (Keep chilled until ready to use.)

4. Roll out dough to 1/8-inch thickness on a floured surface. Cut into 2-inch squares or use the rim of a drinking glass or cookie cutter to cut out 2-inch circles.

5. Place dough shapes on an ungreased cookie sheet; top with desired pie filling (or dried apricots like my mom used to use—see alternate instructions!), and fold 2 opposite corners together. Use a bit of water on your fingertip to make sure they stick.

6. Bake in a 350-degree oven for 12 minutes, or until cookies are lightly browned. Remove cookies from cookie sheet; cool on a wire rack.

Drizzle

1 c. sifted powdered sugar   2 tbsp. water or orange juice

Blend together powdered sugar and water. Use a spoon to apply drizzle in a tight zig-zag motion over the cooled foldovers.

Apricot alternative

Ingredients:

2   6-oz. package dried apricots

½ c. brandy
1 c. sifted powdered sugar

Instructions:

1. Soak apricots in brandy for 1 hour or overnight. Drain; reserving liquid; pat apricots dry.

2. Combine 1 cup sifted powdered sugar and 2 to 3 tablespoons of reserved apricot brandy to make icing.

3. Follow instructions above to make cookies, using apricots as filling.

4. Dip half of each cookie in icing.

As a kid, I never understood why my mom was so drawn to sunshine and soil, but now that I'm older, I know firsthand that warm dirt feels just like possibilities. I understand that for my mom, going into the garden was going home. It was improving a piece of the world—humanity's and our own.

As I was typing that last line, a huge white egret captured my attention as it flew past my second-story window. I watched it travel, like a long-drawn note, across the solitude of our wide backyard sky. The sun is starting to set now, and everything out there is bathed in liquid gold, including the egret, now out of view and likely on its way to capture the attention of someone else.

What I just experienced is called **soft fascination**.[2] Isn't that beautiful? It means "attention that requires no effort" and it allows us to do two very curative things at once: experience beauty and dream. It gives us an opportunity to feel restored *and* reflect or make decisions, and that combination can really alleviate stress.

> Caught myself staring at the sparkling sunlight in a bucket of water and later just standing in the garden taking in the scent of warming earth.
>
> —WILLIAM PAUL WINCHESTER

Hard fascination, on the other hand, prevents us from thinking about anything except the thing we are looking at. It's highly stimulating and requires our undivided attention. Think sporting events, watching TV, or scrolling on your phone. It may feel like a satisfying distraction temporarily, but it doesn't seem to have the same long-term restorative benefits that soft fascination does.

In the weeks following my panic attack in 2018, the only place I felt even *kind of* okay was on our front porch. I didn't know exactly why it was so comforting at the time, but the summertime scent of sweet olive in the air was like a balm for my weary soul, and the wind chimes gently clinking near our front door gave my restless mind something soothing to hold on to. Now I know that sometimes coming home is soft fascination.

> Back in medieval Europe, the earliest hospitals were monastic infirmaries; the garden was often at the center of the complex, its plants and presence a key part of the healing process.
>
> —SALLY COULTHARD

Soft fascination is a gift. It was created to help us recover. And it's not just an oxygen mask marked "in case of emergency" for when we're in the thick of it. It's a tool that can help us catch our breath *all the time*. Again, it isn't going to solve all our problems, but it can create room in our hearts to feel grateful, and gratefulness will always be an important step toward peace. Don't skip it by jumping ahead for instant relief. Don't miss out on the chance to deeply heal. Soft fascination works because it's a direct connection to precious and peaceful you.

> Celebrate the varied splendour in this world, and remind yourself that it can also be found in *you*.
>
> —DR. SALMA FAROOK

biophilia

noun | ˌbī-ō-ˈfi-lē-ə

An innate desire or biological drive to preserve oneself by communing with nature.[3]

Things I Love

- the sound of birdsong
- cotton-ball clouds in a cerulean blue sky
- the tickle of tree leaves in the breeze
- birds on a wire
- that moist-earth fragrance
- the bright, silvery-white sparkle of Venus (did you know it's the second brightest natural object in the night sky after the moon? I look for it almost every night!)
- water with sun glitter on its surface
- the crunch of gravel underfoot
- lichen-covered bark and rocks
- an evening sparked by fireflies
- snow-white sand between my toes
- the scent of wood smoke in air so crisp you can snap it
- a giant white egret, unexpectedly sailing by

SOME of MY FAVORITE QUOTES about NATURE

There is another alphabet, whispering from every leaf, singing from every river, shimmering from every sky.

—DEJAN STOJANOVIC

• • •

If you go to a place on anything but your own feet you are taken there too fast, and miss a thousand delicate joys that were waiting for you by the wayside.

—ELIZABETH VON ARNIM

• • •

I wonder if the snow loves the trees and fields, that it kisses them so gently? And then it covers them up snug, you know, with a white quilt; and perhaps it says, "Go to sleep, darlings, till the summer comes again."

—LEWIS CARROLL

I felt my lungs inflate with the onrush of scenery—air, mountains, trees, people. I thought, "This is what it is to be happy."

—SYLVIA PLATH

• • •

The best remedy for those who are afraid, lonely or unhappy is to go outside, somewhere where they can be quite alone with the heavens, nature and God. Because only then does one feel that all is as it should be and that God wishes to see people happy, amidst the simple beauty of nature. As long as this exists, and it certainly always will, I know that then there will always be comfort for every sorrow, whatever the circumstances may be. And I firmly believe that nature brings solace in all troubles.

—ANNE FRANK

A quiet secluded life in the country, with the possibility of being useful to people to whom it is easy to do good, and who are not accustomed to have it done to them; then work which one hopes may be of some use; then rest, nature, books, music, love for one's neighbor—such is my idea of happiness.

—Leo Tolstoy

• • •

Whenever there is a breeze in the old forest, you might, for a moment, realize that the trees are singing. There, on the wind, are the voices of sugarberry and juniper and maple.

—Kathi Appelt

• • •

It is only when we are aware of the earth and of the earth as poetry that we truly live.

—Henry Beston

I am never so conscious of living on a planet and journeying through the universe as when walking on the familiar path which leads from my front porch out past the cow barn, through the gate into the pasture, and down to the pond.

—William Paul Winchester

• • •

Landscapes of great wonder and beauty lie under our feet and all around us. They are discovered in tunnels in the ground, the heart of flowers, the hollows of trees, fresh-water ponds, seaweed jungles between tides, and even drops of water. Life in these hidden worlds is more startling in reality than anything we can imagine. How could this earth of ours, which is only a speck in the heavens, have so much variety of life, so many curious and exciting creatures?

—Walt Disney

In still moments by the sea life seems large-drawn and simple. It is there we can see into ourselves.

—ROLF EDBERG

. . .

Live in each season as it passes; breathe the air, drink the drink, taste the fruit, and resign yourself to the influence of the earth.

—HENRY DAVID THOREAU

When you feel overwhelmed by a stressful situation or a physical sensation. When you feel lost— like you're racing against a clock to get to a place that may or may not even exist—let this serve as a reminder that you are like a seed. Full of potential and designed to adapt, and learn, and grow. You are an ever-changing universe in and of yourself. So soften to your surroundings and trust that you were built to blossom. Know that there is magic inside you no matter which side of the soil you're on.

—LAYLA PALMER

coming home is . . .

curiosity

I wonder all the time about who I would be if I didn't have to be so vigilant all the time, and I really want to meet that person, and I really want her to be able to succeed. Because right now I feel like my creative brain gets really shrunken, because I spend so much time thinking about how to keep myself safe and I want to know who I would be if I didn't have to think about safety all the time. That person could do so many things. That curiosity, meeting her, really knowing her, keeps me going.

—Chanel Miller

When I first started to struggle with overwhelming anxiety, no one mentioned the importance of curiosity. I'm not talking about the wracking-your-brain-for-answers kind of curious. No, I'm pointing to a curiosity that is open to the possibility of growth, not just hyper-fixated on rickety predictions. Because here's the thing about predictions: We stink at making them. We are literally the only life form on our planet that has the ability to use reason that way, but nine times out of ten, we are *way* off when it comes to correctly guessing how something will actually pan out. Psychologists call it **impact bias**, and it describes our tendency to overestimate the intensity or duration of our future emotions and states of feeling.

A few years ago, psychologists studying impact bias invited a group of people with generalized anxiety disorder to write down whatever they were currently worrying about. The subjects did it every day for two weeks, and by the end of the study, 85 percent of what the group had been worried about never actually happened or led to a positive outcome—the complete opposite of what they had predicted. 79 percent of the remaining 15 percent said they either discovered they could handle the negative outcome better than they expected or that the negative outcome actually taught them a lesson worth learning. In other words, that means the "prediction machines" in 97 percent of the group were not reliable.[1]

Now, obviously, not worrying is easier said than done, but studies like this one prove that what we worry about is usually not much more than our fearful thoughts harassing us with unreliable ideas—and that worrying about an outcome is almost never indicative of how it is actually going to turn out.

Prediction Machine

> "I'm trying to fix my pain with certainty, as if I'm one right choice away from relief. I'm stuck in anxiety quicksand: The harder I try to climb my way out, the lower I sink. The only way to survive is to make no sudden movements, to get comfortable with discomfort, and to find peace without answers."
>
> —GLENNON DOYLE MELTON

So how do we break the worry habit? Or as Kevin would say, how do we disconnect from certain feelings and behaviors on a Tuesday morning? One helpful way is to keep a curious mindset. Again, it isn't always easy, and replacing a worry habit with a curiosity habit does take consistent effort and time, but I am getting better at softening to some of the tension that comes along with being unsure by accepting that I am not an expert. No one is. Not even the people who are really good at (intentionally or unintentionally) making us feel bad about worrying. ☺

In other words, by ragdoll-ing our minds and our responses, we release some of our rigid expectations. We open ourselves up to the possibility that there might be more than one end result, and in turn, we are propelled a little closer to that probability. With a curious mindset, we aren't held hostage by so many whys and what-ifs; we're fueled naturally by the intrigue of what comes next. And when it comes to overcoming adversity of any kind, what we decide to do next will always be very important.

But what does keeping a curious mindset look like on a Tuesday morning? For me, it often looks like approaching indecision with the answer to this question: Am I making this choice for Present Moment Layla? Or am I doing this for Future Layla? Meaning, am I avoiding feelings so that I can feel comfortable and safe right now, in the present moment? Or am I choosing to step into a little discomfort today, so that Future Layla will have proof she is safe? Either way, there will be a price to pay, so the question is: Am I willing to pay that price right now, or am I going to make Future Layla pay it later?

By ever-so-gently pushing your boundaries that way, you can build a powerful arsenal of evidence. One that will help you remember the things you forget so quickly when life gets hard. One that puts things into perspective and reminds you that you are brave, that you were created to contribute, and that you can do so-called impossible things.

So if you are clenched—paralyzed at the intersection of feeling and doing—remind yourself (often) to open up and soften. Be, as Pat Conroy writes, "like a folding chair let out by the pool."[2] Doing so will create room to improve, and you need that kind of space to do anything other than just exist. Things like insecurity, anxiety, grief, and pain may be a part of us, but they definitely don't have to define us or hold us back.

> You have to unfurl your wings in order to give the winds of change a chance to carry you.
>
> —LAYLA PALMER

Let's try not to forget that...

When you reach for the stars, you are reaching for the farthest thing out there. When you reach deep into yourself, it is the same thing, but in the opposite direction. If you reach in both directions, you will have spanned the universe.

—Vera Nazarian

• • •

You never know what's around the corner. It could be everything. Or it could be nothing. You keep putting one foot in front of the other, and then one day you look back and you've climbed a mountain.

—Tom Hiddleston

• • •

I have told you these things, so that in me you may have peace. In this world you will have trouble. But take heart! I have overcome the world.

—John 16:33 niv

Sometimes it's important to work for that pot of gold. But other times it's essential to take time off and to make sure that your most important decision of the day simply consists of choosing which color to slide down on the rainbow.

—Douglas Pagels

• • •

You were not made to be grounded. You need the crisp air, a belly full of laughter, a heart carrying so much love you feel the seams stretching.

Mostly, you need to realize that one by one the population has swelled to billions, but even still you were hand selected, all beauty and flaw, to never be replicated.

—Tyler Kent White

Coming back to where you started is not the same as never leaving.

—Terry Pratchett

• • •

Success is not final, failure is not fatal: it is the courage to continue that counts.

—Anonymous

• • •

There is always some beauty left—in nature, sunshine, freedom, in yourself; these can all help you.

—Anne Frank

• • •

Wherever you are in your development, whatever you are doing, with a strong affirmation of all your goodness and good deeds, with a gentle understanding of your weakness, God is forever loving you.

You do not have to change, grow, or be good in order to be loved. Rather you are loved so that you can change, grow, and be good.

—John Joseph Powell

Once the storm is over, you won't remember how you made it through, how you managed to survive. You won't even be sure, whether the storm is really over. But one thing is certain. When you come out of the storm, you won't be the same person who walked in. That's what this storm's all about.

—Haruki Murakami

• • •

Worrying is carrying tomorrow's load with today's strength—carrying two days at once. It is moving into tomorrow ahead of time. Worrying doesn't empty tomorrow of its sorrow, it empties today of its strength.

—Corrie ten Boom

• • •

The best antidote I know for worry is work. The best cure for weariness is the challenge of helping someone who is even more tired. One of the great ironies of life is this: He or she who serves almost always benefits more than he or she who is served.

—Gordon B. Hinckley

Peace of mind is that mental condition in which you have accepted the worst.

—LIN YUTANG

• • •

We waste so much energy trying to cover up who we are when beneath every attitude is the want to be loved, and beneath every anger is a wound to be healed and beneath every sadness is the fear that there will not be enough time. When we hesitate in being direct, we unknowingly slip something on, some added layer of protection that keeps us from feeling the world, and often that thin covering is the beginning of a loneliness which, if not put down, diminishes our chances of joy. It's like wearing gloves every time we touch something, and then, forgetting we chose to put them on, we complain that nothing feels quite real. Our challenge each day is not to get dressed to face the world but to unglove ourselves so that the doorknob feels cold and the car handle feels wet and the kiss goodbye feels like the lips of another being, soft and unrepeatable.

—MARK NEPO

It's never too late or, in my case, too early to be whoever you want to be. There's no time limit, stop whenever you want. You can change or stay the same, there are no rules to this thing. We can make the best or the worst of it. I hope you make the best of it. And I hope you see things that startle you. I hope you feel things you never felt before. I hope you meet people with a different point of view. I hope you live a life you're proud of. If you find that you're not, I hope you have the courage to start all over again.

—ERIC ROTH

coming home is . . .
childlike wonder

what you do with your attention is, in the end, what you do with your life.

—John Green

From my second-story window I can see freshly washed linens snapping in the breeze, an impressive, old row of giant sugarberry trees, and towering thunderheads building in the afternoon sky—a reminder that here in the south, even the clearest of summer days can end in a downpour. But those kinds of clouds almost always collapse before the sun begins to set, and for that I am grateful, because wide, cinnabar skies are on my list of favorite things about this place too.

We bought our place in August 2021, after searching for several months online. My mother-in-law wanted to live closer to her friends, appointments, and activities in town, and Kevin and I dreamed of finding a hobby farm closer to that same city. It seemed like a pretty tall order at the time—I mean, the housing market was upside down, and how many farms are conveniently located and include a dedicated in-law suite? Nevertheless, I shared our wish list on social media, and wouldn't you know it, a follow-alonger named Tammy was kind enough to send me an email titled, "Country house in the city" with a link to this listing.

The very first aerial photo had me at hello. I immediately texted Kevin, and we were standing in the front yard thirty minutes later. The wide-ranging meadows were even more magical at eye level, and I could've kissed every trunk on the tree-lined gravel drive. There were nearly six sprawling acres for whatever tickled our fancy, and although we had never

Photo by Ryan Sexton

Country house in city ⊅ Inbox ×

Tammy
to me ▾

Tue, Jun 15, 2021, 10:09 PM

https://www.zillow.com/homedetails/

Sent from my iPhone

↩ Reply   → Forward

"Enjoy country living in the city limits with this traditional two-story brick home with over 4500 square feet nestled on nearly 6 acres!! Plenty of room to roam inside and out with five spacious bedrooms, large living room with soaring ceilings and captivating wood burning fireplace, relaxing Florida room, in law suite with walk in shower, formal dining room, and versatile room perfect for an office or sitting room. Fantastic master suite with two full bathrooms, separate vanities, three walk in closets and tiled laundry room with abundant cabinets and storage. Nice sized bedrooms upstairs all with ample closet space and two full baths. New Roof and New Pool liner. 30x30 metal barn with plenty of room for equipment. Kitchen features newly installed range hood with eat in area offering a picturesque backyard view out the bay window. Come see all this home has to offer!"

cared for so much land before, the possibilities seemed endless. As we wandered around the property, the hard edges of any intrusive thoughts were smoothed by soft fascination. I imagined a vegetable patch and some fruit trees, definitely a few barnyard animals. I assumed lilacs wouldn't survive, what with all the heat and humidity in summer, but I thought surely we could grow some strawberries. I envisioned a limewashed exterior on the house and string lights above a European-style courtyard out back. Maybe even a vintage goods shop or rotating art gallery in the large, metal barn that split the tree line in two.

The house itself wasn't exactly what I had in mind, but it felt so familial and comfortable—it just needed a little TLC. And like I said, I'm no stranger to home improvement. I come from a long line of DIY-ers, and pouring into a house has always felt like a filling-up of me. There were enough bedrooms and bathrooms for everyone, and yeah, they were empty and outdated, but even without furniture, the house just felt like home. I think everyone who toured it with us that week could feel its layers of warmth and sweetness.

> I wanted to hold onto the house the way you'd hold onto a love letter.
>
> —OTTESSA MOSHFEGH

And would you believe that we came *this close* to not making an offer? It's true. We got cold feet thinking about all the moving parts involved in buying and selling, but Kevin's mom gave us the nudge we needed to go for it, and our offer was accepted that June. Our former home sold a few weeks later, and we were all moved into the new (old) place in August.

> Farmette: A small area of land used for backyard animals with a modest garden; a hobby farm or country home that serves as an intentional lifestyle not a main source of income.
>
> —EMILY BRUNO

Our property backs up to eight-hundred-some acres of undisturbed land, where large clusters of cows manage the pasture year-round. A shallow band of woodland separates our back meadow from their expansive pasture. There is one place in particular that is fairly easy to traverse—almost like the previous owner must have cut a path at one point. I feel like I'm twelve years old again every time I wander through. It's funny how finding just enough room to travel through a labyrinth of branches can turn a trip through the woods into such an unexpected gift, ya know?

> What if you could change the scenes happening around you just by moving your legs in a certain way? You can. It's called "walking."
>
> —SHUNYA

I've experienced a lot of that ordinary-turned-extraordinary magic here since we moved in. I don't think it's specifically linked to this (or any) particular place; I just think I'm on more of a mission to notice it. I'm more devoted to prioritizing curiosity. After so much turbulence and time to process, I feel more determined than ever to change the way I think about my life, and for me, a fresh start felt like an important part of doing that. I think I went through a kind of "wintering" at our previous place. I learned some things about enduring the cold and that, sometimes, a move can feel like a spring.

> Your life is sometimes a stone in you, and then, a star.
> —MAGGIE STIEFVATER

Anxiety-related adversity is still a strong wind, but I feel more in tune with the truth now, and with this place that feels like a natural next chapter. One that's not only waiting to be written, but also one that's waiting to be read. One full of magical things patiently waiting for me. Because I can't tell you how many times I've flown down the stairs and thrown on my rubber boots, then carefully waded across a carpet of knee-high grass to get a closer look at a "bunny," only to discover that it's actually a massive anthill made of silty clay. Or squeezed my body between once-taut, now noodle-y lengths of rusty barbed wire to see what a black-eyed Susan looks like up close. Where there was once just lint or the occasional folded-up receipt, now my pockets also hold unshelled peanuts (for the Sherman's fox squirrel we call Surly) and my growing collection of heart-shaped rocks.

This past April, after everything around it had turned green, I spotted a giant froth of white blossoms bursting from what appeared to be a large tree reaching across the barbed wire fence out back. I dropped what I was doing so I could race across the meadow to meet it, and while I can no longer recall what that even was, the experience of being surprised by that tree and subsequently setting off in its direction is now as much a part of me as the feet that took me to it. As I stood beneath the architecture of its wide-sweeping

BECAUSE WHEN YOU FIND A
POSTCARD FROM 1891 ON EBAY
SENT BY THE MAN WHO NAMED
THE TREE IN YOUR BACK PASTURE—
YOU BUY IT!

limbs—its tiny ivory flowers "forming a miracle of lace against the heavens"[1]—I felt so lucky to know that it was living in our backyard. It was as though I had not only purchased a plot, I had also inherited the long-breathing history of an extraordinary and capable seed. The now-ness of it all helped me to feel fully present.

Things like that always do . . . if we let them. The trick is to keep asking yourself *what's interesting about this thing?* Because peace flows on the electricity of the present and child-like wonder always holds so much voltage. I must have stood there for ten whole minutes just admiring it. *Is it older than I am? Is it wild, or did someone plant it?* If only trees could talk! Its willowy branches were so spellbinding, swooping out in every direction, bouncing in the breeze underneath their weight in white. I didn't know its name, but a plant-identifying app on my phone formally introduced us a few days later.

"Layla, meet Mexican Plum. She was named in the late 1800s by a fascinating fella named Sereno Watson and dons fragrant, showy white flowers before its green leaves and small, purplish-red plums begin to appear. And, yes, you can eat them."

"Mexican Plum, meet Layla. She lives in the big brick house over yonder and sure appreciates your presence back here."

But again, I am *not* saying you need to put your house on the market and move somewhere different to create a clean slate and be free of your problems. That never works. You can't outrun yourself. I'm just saying, keep an eye on your buckets. Meaning, if the one labeled "childlike wonder" is mostly just draining, coming home can look like carving out time to refill it.

The real you is still a little child who never grew up. Sometimes that little child comes out when you are having fun or playing, when you feel happy, when you are painting, or writing poetry, or playing the piano, or expressing yourself *in some way. These are the happiest moments of your life—when the real you comes out, when you don't care about the past and you don't worry about the future.*

—DON MIGUEL RUIZ

I heard author Chanel Miller tell a childlike wonder-related story one time, and I've been pointing people to it ever since. It's such a great example of the power of noticing. She said she was riding the subway one time when she saw two guys sitting next to each other sharing a cluster of grapes. One of them had a smiley face patch on his sweatpants, and the other suddenly cracked them both up by exclaiming, "*Nom! Nom! Nom!*" while "feeding" one of his grapes to the mouth on the patch. Chanel said, "the friend in the sweatpants was laughing so hard he couldn't breathe and their little game became: pressing the little grape to the mouth, and then the other one would just lose it. Like, that was the whole ride."[2]

But here's what else I love: That was Chanel's *whole ride* too. Her brain was inside their game, and in being present enough to notice *their* joy, she opened herself up to a whole ride full of it too. I mean, can't you just picture the smile on her face? Now can't you just picture the smile on my face as I sit here and type it all out for you? (I hope you're smiling now too!) Chanel said it best when, after she finished telling that story, she added, "The world is full of that stuff. And it's free and it's happening all the time. And you just gotta—if you are stuck in your little toilet paper roll of depression—redirect that little roll to those small moments. They're not going to save you, but I swear if you string them along, you come out somewhere different."[3]

> I do believe in an everyday sort of magic—the inexplicable connectedness we sometimes experience with places, people, works of art and the like.
>
> —CHARLES DE LINT

I would even go so far as to say you come out closer to home. The home of who you are, I mean. Because childlike wonder can go such a long way when it comes to dissolving one's discomfort zone and expanding one's life.

> Some days you must learn a great deal. But you should also have days when you allow what is already in you to swell up and touch everything.
>
> —E. L. KONIGSBURG

And Chanel is right. That kind of magic *is* happening everywhere. And it's okay if we don't always have it in us to go out and look for it. It's just as accessible from down in the dumps. Maybe even more so. Because that kind of joy doesn't require positive thinking, or extra effort, or even your full attention. It just happens. You discover a new-to-you fruit tree at the edge of your yard because it blooms a totally different color. You notice two guys laughing uncontrollably at a smiley patch eating grapes. Don't cut yourself off from that stuff. Allow yourself to soften to a more panoramic kind of attention. One that's less judgmental and more accepting. Make a conscious decision to look at things one of two ways: as if you are seeing them for the very first time, or as if you are seeing them for the very last time. Make noticing a part of your breathing, and follow the air as it leads you back home.

Only when we pay attention and notice small moments, do we make the connections that lead to a change in our perspective.

—ANDREA GOEGLEIN

The other day, I was washing my hands in the kitchen. I had been outside dealing with fire ant mounds and there wasn't any hand soap left, so I reached for the liquid dishwashing soap instead. When I tipped the bottle over to dab some onto the palm of my left hand, the seesaw motion sent a poof of tiny, wild bubbles flying up into the air. I watched one of them climb toward the ceiling as I rubbed my hands together in front of the sink. Just before it reached the little white stalactites on the textured ceiling, it stopped short, hovering in place for a moment before it began to quickly drop back down. It met another invisible force field about an inch above the countertop, where it paused again and hovered in place just slightly above it. As if to say, "See? That's how panic works too. It rises up, but then it always retreats."

Or at least that's what I heard.

And when the bubble popped in mid-air, without touching anything around it, I was reminded, once again, that with time, and by floating through it, it's possible for a fear of fear to disappear too.

"IF NOT MINNESOTA, AND NOT ALABAMA, WHERE IS HOME?"

Home is...

THE WARMTH IN OUR SPIRIT
THE WARRIOR IN OUR BONES
THE SUM OF OUR STRATA
THE SOURCE OF OUR DREAMS
A SPARK OF HOPE
A SIGH OF RELIEF
LOVE TRANSMITTED
LOVE RECEIVED
A FOOTHOLD
A CHOICE
ABUNDANT GRACE
RESTORATIVE STORIES
SURRENDERING TO THE CURRENT
EXPLORING THE UNKNOWN
DOWNTIME
QUALITY TIME
TREADING LIGHTLY IN TENDER PLACES
UN-DOING THE WORK
REWRITING THE STORY
AN INVITATION
OLD-FASHIONED GRATIFICATION
SAYING YES
SAYING NO
A COMFORT FOOD
A COMFORT BOOK
CHILDLIKE WONDER
SOFT FASCINATION
REMEMBERING WHO YOU ARE
LEARNING SOMETHING NEW
A PRISMATIC PERSPECTIVE
A THOROUGH REVIEW
THE WARM FUZZIES
A NEW CHAPTER
A ONE-FOOT JOURNEY
A CURIOUS MINDSET
REALIZING YOU'RE NOT LOST
GOD NEVER LETTING GO

The
Beginning.

acknowledgments

I have this fascination with the acknowledgments in the back of books and I'm obsessive about reading them. Sometimes they're pretty standard shout-outs but sometimes they make me feel an incredible surge of feelings. Sometimes I get all choked up. Sometimes they're a whole little story in and of itself. I mean, I think about all the blood, sweat, and tears that go into writing a book, and then I read these beautiful acknowledgements where authors just lay it all out and thank those who made it possible, who encouraged them, who saw it all the way through with them even when they may have doubted it would ever happen. I think it gives me an even deeper level of appreciation of the book I'm holding in my hands. I feel like I get to know the author just a little bit more. They've bared their hearts and soul in their work, and then I get this tiny glimpse more with the acknowledgements.

—Jamie Miller

I FEEL THE SAME WAY! (")

Thank you to my "beacon babes"—Jennifer Dukes Lee, Lisa Jackson, and Lisa-Jo Baker. It was your luminous encouragement and enthusiasm that convinced me to take my castle-in-the-sky and turn it into this bonafide beacon book! I didn't always know where to start (or finish—ha!), so thank you for shoring up the puzzling path and shedding light on all of its mysterious curves and corners. We may have been separated by thousands of miles during our thousand-day adventure, but I took great comfort in knowing you were always a quick email, text, phone call, or walkie-talkie (Voxer) away. I will be forever indebted to you for believing in this project . . . and this person!

Thank you (thank you, thank you!) to the entire Bethany House Publishing team—specifically Andy McGuire, Brian Brunsting, Dan Pitts, Kate Jameson, Sharon Hodge, Mycah McKeown, Rebecca Schriner, Stephanie Smith, Bria Conway, and William Overbeeke. As rock 'n' roller Dave Grohl once put it, "You should be knighted." (Someone go tell the King to add Sir and Dame to their names!) Your guidance, grace, and gusto added so much joy and confidence to the climb, and your contributions to *Coming Home* made it feel so special, and so real, long before it was printed. My deepest thanks for trusting this first-timer with the opportunity of a lifetime!

Thank you, Mom, Dad, Katie, Kerry, Aunt Chriss, and Aubrey. I'm SO glad your contributions are all tucked in here too! You make *Coming Home* better, in more ways than one. My name may be on the spine, but y'all are my backbone, and I am so lucky to have you in my life. ♡

Thank you to my dearest faraway friends, Tacy Riehm and Kyle Campbell. You two are moonlight amid the mountains; you both just have this effortless way of helping people remember to breathe.

Kyle—I felt it from the moment I stumbled onto your Instagram account, @SuddenJourneys. Your photos are so soulful, and having one on the cover of *Coming Home* is, for me, having a literal dream come true. So, thank you for squeezing that charming antique desk and scrumptious bentwood chair into the back of your car and for driving across (four!) county lines to Fontmell Magna. Thank you for following *my* heart to Fiddlesticks (a cottage I've always wanted to visit!), and for stopping in Shaftesbury for fresh flowers along the way. Thank you for bringing the books, and the berries, and the vintage dishes and candles, and for allowing me to arrange them just so via Voxer. ("Just skooch the linen napkin back a liiiiiittle bit more so we can see that yummy, painted wooden drawer knob," "Let's do a couple of runaway berries on the top right corner of the desk," "Let's go with the amber candles instead of the cream ones. I feel like they're more quirky and casual—just like the person who would be sitting at that desk!") Being there "with" you was one of the most exhilarating and meaningful days of my creative life. Thank you, truly, for sharing your time, your talent, and for giving all the feelings in this book a bespoke and magnetic face.

Tacy—*Mwen renmen ou*! Thank you for always making me feel balanced, buoyant, safe, and seen. You're the best darn friend an over-thinker could ask for, and I am so grateful for the way you accept me exactly as I am. We may live on opposite sides of the country, but the memories of our good times and good talks are constantly racing across time to find me, and I can't tell you how many times I thought about you while writing this book. You are a lighthouse. A secret weapon. A wonder woman. I really should make you a cape. ☺

Thanks also to these super-creatives:

Susan Branch, your trilogy of books are the sparks from outside that caught my tinder on fire, and without them, this one certainly wouldn't exist. I am so grateful for the way you encourage readers (and writers!) to marvel and meander. Oh, and thank you for introducing me to the English countryside. I am determined to sail there on the *Queen Mary 2* because of you. Or, at the very least, take the ferry out to "your" tiny island of Martha's Vineyard! ♡

David M. Bird, it was you who inspired my ever-growing list of "fresh-air folks," and it has been such a treat to follow along with you on Instagram. Your ability to turn an acorn into a Becorn is such a special thing to behold, and I'm (not so) secretly hoping you make a SEA-corn next. ☺

Herbie Knott, much like the surprising glow in your photo of "The Old Door at Heligan," you have been such an unexpected glimmer of light! Thank you for responding to my message about including your mesmerizing picture. "Restorative Stories" would not be the same without it!

Ruth Klossner, thank you for taking such good care of those old berry patch negatives and for digging them up all these years later. I won't ever see a strawberry without thinking of you now too.

Billy Pope, you don't just take photos, you make them. Thank you for framing such a meaningful moment in time and for allowing *Coming Home* to forever hold it. (Thanks also to Captain Rene for giving me permission to include Billy's photo of Fiddler!)

Thank you to these present-people: Drew Linsalata (@The _Anxious_Truth), Sharon McMahon (@SharonSaysSo), and Shannan Martin (@ShannanWrites). You may never know exactly how much your friendship, guidance, and generosity have meant to me, so I'm tucking this thank-you here to forever remind you that you are GIFTS. You impacted my life in such a positive way, and I couldn't have finished some of these stories without you. I don't know what I did to deserve the three of you, but I am so grateful for the way you neighbor!

Thank you to my precious IRL friends and to the incredible e-friends who have found their way to this page via "The Lettered Cottage" blog or social media. (Abi, Aimee, Allie, Aly, Alisha, Allyson, Alyssa, Amanda, Amy, Andi, Angie, Angela, Angelica, Anjuli, Ann, Annette, April, Ashlea, Ashley, Aubrie, Bambi, Barb, Barbara, Becca, Bekah, Becky, Belinda, Benton, Beth, Betsy, Bev, Billy, Bobby Jon, Bre, Brenda, Bridget, Brittany, Brooke, Carla, Carlos, Carmen, Cary, Cat, Cathy, Cassandra, Chad, Charlotte, Chastity, Chelsea, Cheryl, Chris, Christie, Christy, Cindy, Clare, Colleen, Cyndi, Dacia, Dahnielle, Danielle, Dana, Danelle, Deanna, Deb, DeLayna, Desiree, Diane, Donal, Donna, Dylan, Elise, Elizabeth, Elle McBee, Ellen, Emily, Emmy, Erika, Erin, Esty, Evan, Faith, Frances, Gail, Glenn, Glenwyn, the Governerds, Gwen, Hannah, Harmony, Hayley, Heather, Holly, Jamie, Janae, Jana, Jane, Jamie, Jeannine, Jen, Jenny, Jeff, Jerica, Jess, Jett, Jimmy, Joanna, Joni, Josh, Joy, Julia, Julie, Karen, Karla, Kate, Katelyn, Kathy, Katie, Keely, Kelly, Kelsi, Kendra, Ki, Kim, Kimberly, Kindrel, Kirsty, Krista, Kristi, Kristin, Lacey, Laura, Lauren, LeeAnn, Leila, Lily, Linda, Lindsey, Liz Marie, Lizzie, Lori, Louise, Lucy, Luke, Lynda, Lynette, Lynn, Maggie, Mallory, Mandy Rose, Maria, Marian, Marianne, Marie, Mary, Mary-Alice, Marynn, Matt, MB, Megan, Meghan, Melani, Melanie, Melody, Meredith, Michael, Michelle, Micia, Mindy, Minnie, Missy, Monica, Myquillyn, Nakia, Nancy, Natalie, Natasha, Nathan, Neada, Necee, Nichol, Nicole, Nikki, Noel, Olivia, Pamela, Rachel, Raftyn, Ree, Renee, Rhoda, Rita-Joy, Robin, Robyn, Ruthie, Salli, Sarah, Shannon, Sara Jo, Sharrah, Shaundra, Shawna, Shelley, Sherri, Sherron, Sherry, Stacy, Stacey, Stephanie, Suzanne, Tammy, Taylor, Thomas, Tiffany, Tiffany-Ann, Tonya, Tori, Traci, Trisha Ann, Victoria, Wendy, and

Wesley, just to name a few!) Thank you for adding value and delight to my life from the other side of the screen and for encouraging me to keep flying by the seat of my (sweat)pants, whether you know you're doing it or not!

Last but not least, thank you to my precious husband, Kevin. I know *Coming Home* was a long and winding road for you, too, and it certainly wouldn't be complete or worth reading without your insightful presence. Thank you for helping me infuse each essay with a wise and warm takeaway, especially on days I struggled to see one. I will forever cherish the countless hours we spent exchanging ideas in the car, across my desk, and along the tree line here at the "farm." (Would it be weird to have our whiteboard bronzed now?) You are the kindest, most patient deep-thinker I have ever met, and building this book (and this life!) with you has been such sweet efflorescence!

notes

1. "I Shall Write a Book," *Selma Times-Journal*, December 31, 1937, page 3. Used with permission.

Introduction

1. Vladimir Nabokov, *Lectures on Literature*, ed. Fredson Bowers (New York: Harcourt, Inc., 1980), 379.
2. Robert Farrar Capon, *The Astonished Heart: Reclaiming the Good News from the Lost-and-Found of Church History* (Grand Rapids, MI: Eerdmans, 1996), 119.

A Note about the Bones of This Book

1. "Efflorescence." *Merriam-Webster's Unabridged Dictionary*, Merriam-Webster, https://unabridged.merriam-webster.com/unabridged/efflorescence.

Chapter 1: Coming Home Is . . . The Warrior in Our Bones

1. David Benioff, *City of Thieves* (New York: Penguin, 2008), 24.
2. Matt Haig, *The Comfort Book* (New York: Penguin, 2021), 193.

Chapter 3: Coming Home Is . . . Surrendering to the Current

1. David Nicholls, *Us* (New York: HarperCollins, 2014), 390.
2. Pierce Brown, *Golden Son* (New York: Del Rey, 2015), 87.
3. Sandy Gingras, *How to Live on an Island* (Harvey Cedars, NJ: Down the Shore Publishing, 2010), 5.
4. Francesca Marciano, *Rules of the Wild* (New York: Vintage Books, 1998), 288.
5. Anthony D'Angelo, *The College Blue Book* (Three Bridges, NJ: Arkad Press, 1995), 79.
6. *Etty: The Letters and Diaries of Etty Hillesum, 1941–1941*, ed. Klaa A.D. Smelik, trans. Arnold J. Pomerans (Grand Rapids, MI: Eerdmans, 2002), 305.

7. "Learning diaphragmatic breathing," Harvard Health Publishing Harvard Medical School, https://www.health.harvard.edu/healthbeat/learning-diaphragmatic-breathing.

Chapter 4: Coming Home Is . . . Restorative Stories

1 Sanober Khan, *A Touch, a Tear, a Tempest* (Allahabad, India: Cyberwit.net, 2012), front matter.

2. Ella Berthoud as quoted in World Economic Forum, "Meet the Woman Prescribing Books as a Cure," *The European Sting*, February 25, 2020, https://europeansting.com/2020/02/25/meet-the-woman-prescribing-books-as-a-cure/.

3. "Timeline," The Lost Gardens of Heligan, https://www.heligan.com/the-story/timeline.

4. Tim Smit in *Back to Eden: The Transformative Power of Plants*, YouTube video, July 26, 2022, 13:00, https://www.youtube.com/watch?v=RRfWODpIFhY.

5. "The Heligan Story," The Lost Gardens of Heligan, heligan.com, https://www.heligan.com/images/uploads/Heligan_map_for_web.pdf.

6. Albert Schweitzer, *Memoirs of Childhood and Youth*, Translated by C.T. Campion (New York: Macmillan, 1931), 190.

7. Jeff Zentner, Goodbye Days (New York: Ember, 2017), 88.

8. Jennifer Palmer, "Now More Than Ever, Nature Has Valuable Lessons to Teach Us, NEEF, https://www.neefusa.org/nature/land/now-more-ever-nature-has-valuable-lessons-teach-us.

9. Dr. Julie Smith, *Why Has Nobody Told Me This Before?* (HarperSanFrancisco, 2022), 185.

Chapter 5: Coming Home Is . . . A New Chapter

1 Diana Gabaldon, *Dragonfly in Amber* (New York: Dell, 1993), 55.

2. Sharon Kay Penman, *When Christ and His Saints Slept* (New York: Henry Holt and Company, 1995), 612.

3. Suzanne Finnamore, *The Zygote Chronicles* (New York: Grove Press, 2002), 14.

4. Parker J. Palmer, *Let Your Life Speak: Listening for the Voice of Vocation* (San Francisco: Jossey-Bass, 2000), 93–94, bold emphasis added.

Chapter 6: Coming Home Is . . . Undoing the Work

1. Sebastian Faulks, *Charlotte Gray* (New York: Vintage, 2000), 66.

2. Roy T. Bennett, T*he Light in the Heart: Inspirational Thoughts for Living Your Best Life* (Roy Bennet, 2016), 57.

3. Erik Pevernagie, from the description for his painting "Voices of the Sea," http://www.pevernagie.com/index.php?option=com_rsgallery2&page=inline&gid=4&limit=1&Itemid=6&limitstart=22.

4. Alina Tugend, "Praise Is Fleeting, but Brickbats We Recall," New York Times, March 23, 2012, http://www.pevernagie.com/index.php?option=com_rsgallery2&page=inline&gid=4&limit=1&Itemid=6&limitstart=22.

5. Tugend, "Praise Is Fleeting."

6. Jonathan M. Adler as quoted in Tory Rodriguez, "Negative Emotions Are Key to Well-Being," Scientific American, May 1, 2013, https://www.scientificamerican.com/article/negative-emotions-key-well-being/.

7. White Plains Hospital, "My Doctor Told Me to Get Outside!," Health Matters, January 28, 2021, https://healthmatters.wphospital.org/blog/january/2021/my-doctor-told-me-to-get-outside/.

8. Rachel Moss, "Sunshine Improves Mental Wellbeing, with Dark Months Linked to Emotional Distress, Study Finds," Huffpost UK, April 11, 2016, https://www.huffingtonpost.co.uk/entry/how-sun-light-affects-mental-health_uk_581c4f1ce4b09d57a9a8377f#:~:text=According%20to%20scientists%20at%20Brigham,improved%20during%20the%20lightest%20seasons.

9. Moss, "Sunshine Improves Mental Wellbeing."

10. National Recreation and Park Association, "Parks and Improved Mental Health and Quality of Life," National Recreation and Park Association, https://www.nrpa.org/our-work/Three-Pillars/health-wellness/ParksandHealth/fact-sheets/parks-improved-mental-health-quality-life/#:~:text=More%20time%20spent%20in%20parks,of%20life%20for%20your%20community.

11. Peter Dockrill, "Just Looking at Photos of Nature Could Be Enough to Lower Your Work Stress Levels," Science Alert, March 23, 2016, https://www.sciencealert.com/just-looking-at-photos-of-nature-could-be-enough-to-lower-your-work-stress-levels.

12. Wendy Suzuki, "A Neuroscientist Shares the 4 Brain-Changing Benefits of Exercise—and How Much She Does Every Week," CNBC Make It, October 22, 2021, https://www.cnbc.com/2021/10/22/neuroscientist-shares-the-brain-health-benefits-of-exercise-and-how-much-she-does-a-week.html.

13. Gretchen Reynolds, "The Benefits of Exercising Outdoors," New York Times, February 21, 2013, https://archive.nytimes.com/well.blogs.nytimes.com/2013/02/21/the-benefits-of-exercising-outdoors/.

14. Maile Proctor, "6 Science-Backed Ways Being Kind Is Good for Your Health," Quiet Revolution, https://quietrev.com/6-science-backed-ways-being-kind-is-good-for-your-health/.

15. David Hamilton, "The 5 Side Effects of Kindness," *Dr. David R. Hamilton*, May 30, 2011, https://drdavidhamilton.com/the-5-side-effects-of-kindness/.

16. Michael Baraz and Michele Lilyanna, Awakening Joy for Kids (Berkeley, CA: Parallax Press, 2016), 33.

17. "Water, Depression, and Anxiety," *Solara Mental Health*, https://solaramentalhealth.com/can-drinking-enough-water-help-my-depression-and-anxiety/#:~:text=Dehydration%20increases%20stress%20in%20your%20body.&text=Dehydration%20is%20the%20number%20one,and%20stress%20can%20cause%20dehydration.

18. "Water, Depression, and Anxiety," *Solara Mental Health*.

19. "The Importance of Hydration," *Harvard T.H. Chan*, https://www.hsph.harvard.edu/news/hsph-in-the-news/the-importance-of-hydration/#:~:tcxt=Being%20well%2Dhydrated%20also%20improves,woman%20and%2016%20for%20men.

20. Divya Jacob, Pharm, D. "How Much Water Should You Drink Based on Your Weight?", *MedicineNet*, https://www.medicinenet.com/how_much_water_to_drink_based_on_your_weight/article.htm.

Chapter 7: Coming Home Is . . . Instant Old-Fashioned Gratification

1. Terri Windling, "Inspiration . . . and Return," *Myth & Moor*, July 20, 2012, https://www.terriwindling.com/blog/2012/07/patti-smith.html.

2. Wim Wenders, "An Attempted Description of an Indescribable Film," *The Criterion Channel*, November 2, 2009, https://www.criterion.com/current/posts/1289-an-attempted-description-of-an-indescribable-film.

3. Jocelyn Brand and Evan P. Schneider, "Stop Trying to Be Creative," *People Science*, January 25, 2019, https://peoplescience.maritz.com/Articles/2019/stop-trying-to-be-creative.

4. George Land and Beth Jarman, *Breakpoint and Beyond: Mastering the Future—Today* (HarperBusiness, 1992).

5. Aaron Browder, "Children Are Born Creative," *The Open School*, February 19, 2020, https://www.openschooloc.com/2020/02/19/children-are-born-creative/.

6. August Turak, "Can Creativity Be Taught?," *Forbes*, May 22, 2011, https://www.forbes.com/sites/augustturak/2011/05/22/can-creativity-be-taught/?sh=5244ac451abb.

7. Zig Ziglar, *Born to Win* by (Made For Success Publishing, 2017), 148.

Chapter 8: Coming Home Is . . . An Invitation

1. Shauna Niequist, *Cold Tangerines: Celebrating the Extraordinary Nature of Everyday Life* (Grand Rapids, MI: Zondervan, 2020), 233.

2. Lisa Kleypas, *Blue-Eyed Devil* (New York: St. Martin's Press, 2008), 296.

Chapter 10: Coming Home Is . . . Rewriting the Story

1. Rainer Maria Rilke, *Letters to a Young Poet* (Snowball Publishing, 2012), 13.

2. Dr. Claire Weekes, *Hope and Help for Your Nerves: End Anxiety Now* (New York: Signet, 1990), 2.

3. Weekes, *Hope and Help for Your Nerves*, 3.

4. "unplumbed," *The Free Dictionary* by Farlex (Farlex, 2003–2022), https://www.thefreedictionary.com/unplumbed.

5. "unsuspected," *Merriam-Webster Dictionary* (Merriam-Webster, 2022), https://www.merriam-webster.com/dictionary/unsuspected#:~:text=adjective,an%20unsuspected%20illness.

6. David Scott Yeager, Julio Garcia, Patti Brzustoski, William T. Hessert, Valerie Purdie-Vaughns, Nancy Apfel, Allison Master, Matthew E. Williams, and Geoffrey L. Cohen, "Breaking the Cycle of Mistrust: Wise Interventions to Provide Critical Feedback Across the Racial Divide," Journal of Experimental Psychology: General 143, no. 2 (2014): 804–824.

7. Benjamin Hardy, *Personality Isn't Permanent: Break Free from Self-Limiting Beliefs and Rewrite Your Story* (New York: Portfolio/Penguin, 2020), 112.

Chapter 11: Coming Home Is . . . A Choice

1. Jay W. Marks, MD, "Definition of Neuroplasticity," RxList, https://www.rxlist.com/neuroplasticity/definition.htm.

2. Drew Linsalata, *The Anxious Truth: A Step-by-Step Guide to Understanding and Overcoming Panic, Anxiety, and Agoraphobia* (Drew Linsalata, 2020), 135–142.

Chapter 12: Coming Home Is . . . Treading Lightly through Tender Places

1. John Lennon as quoted in Kai Green, "Still Shining On! Remembering John Lennon With 65 of His Most Famous and Profound Quotes," *Parade*, November 25, 2021, https://parade.com/1299046/kaigreen/john-lennon-quotes/.

Chapter 13: Coming Home Is . . . Soft Fascination

1. From Nancy Byrd Turner, "Home," in *Good Housekeeping*, 1925. Used with permission.

2. Avik Basu, Jason Duvall, and Rachel Kaplan, "Attention Restoration Theory: Exploring the Role of Soft Fascination and Mental Bandwidth," *Environment and Behavior* volume 51, issue 9–10 (2019): 1055–1081, https://doi.org/10.1177/0013916518774400.

3. Kara Rogers, "biophilia hypothesis," *Encyclopedia Britannica*, June 25, 2019, https://www.britannica.com/science/biophilia-hypothesis.

Chapter 14: Coming Home Is . . . Curiosity

1. Lucas LaFreniere and Michelle Newman, "Exposing Worry's Deceit: Percentage of Untrue Worries in Generalized Anxiety Disorder Treatment," *Behavior Therapy* volume 51, issue 3 (May 2020): 413–423, doi:10.1016/j.beth.2019.07.003.

2. Pat Conroy, *Beach Music* (New York: Dial Press, 2009), 117.

Chapter 15: Coming Home Is . . . Childlike Wonder

1. Janet Miles, "Two Trees" *Images of Women in Transition*, comp. Janice Grana (Winona, MN: Saint Mary's Press of Minnesota, 1991), 58.

2. Chanel Miller, *We Can Do Hard Things* with Glennon Doyle podcast, "Chanel Miller Promises: We are Never Stuck," May 2, 2022.

3. Miller, *We Can Do Hard Things*.

LAYLA PALMER was artsy from the start(sy) and always dreamed of working with words and whimsy when she grew up. She's been sharing inspiration online since 2008, and she feels most alive when she's creating, exploring, and making people laugh. In 2021, she and her husband, Kevin, coauthored *The Happy Crab,* a children's book about selflessness. *Coming Home* is her first big-kid book.

 @letteredcottage   theletteredcottage.net